SÁNDOR FERENCZI–ERNEST JONES

The History of Psychoanalysis Series

Professor Brett Kahr and Professor Peter L. Rudnytsky (Series Editors)
Published and distributed by Karnac Books

Other titles in the Series

Her Hour Come Round at Last: A Garland for Nina Coltart
edited by Peter L. Rudnytsky and Gillian Preston

Rescuing Psychoanalysis from Freud and Other Essays in Re-Vision
by Peter L. Rudnytsky

Ferenczi and His World: Rekindling the Spirit of the Budapest School
edited by Judit Szekacs-Weisz and Tom Keve

Freud in Zion: Psychoanalysis ad the Making of Modern Jewish Identity
by Eran J. Rolnik

Ferenczi for our Time: Theory and Practice
edited by Judit Szekacs-Weisz and Tom Keve

The Clinic and the Context: Historical Essays
by Elisabeth Young-Bruehl

SÁNDOR FERENCZI–ERNEST JONES

Letters 1911–1933

edited by

Ferenc Erős, Judit Szekacs-Weisz, and Ken Robinson

Routledge
Taylor & Francis Group
LONDON AND NEW YORK

First published 2013 by Karnac Books Ltd.

Published 2018 by Routledge
2 Park Square, Milton Park, Abingdon, Oxon OX14 4RN
711 Third Avenue, New York, NY 10017, USA

Routledge is an imprint of the Taylor & Francis Group, an informa business

British Library Cataloguing in Publication Data

A C.I.P. for this book is available from the British Library

ISBN 9781780491769 (pbk)

Ferenczi letters translated from German by Beate Schumacher

Edited, designed and produced by The Studio Publishing Services Ltd
www.publishingservicesuk.co.uk
e-mail: studio@publishingservicesuk.co.uk

CONTENTS

ACKNOWLEDGEMENTS

The publication of the Ferenczi–Jones correspondence is the result of a professional team working together since 2004. The list of contributors is long, but their work was essential in producing this book. Here, we would like to thank Melinda Friedrich, a PhD student in psychoanalytic history and German philology, who transcribed Ferenczi's German handwritten letters and also worked on the notes for the Hungarian edition. The transcribed text in German (and in Hungarian translation by Petrik Bottka) was first published in a special issue of the review *Thalassa* in 2008. The transcription and the notes were later reviewed by Ernst Falzeder (Salzburg), while the notes were further developed and completed by Ken Robinson (London). Based on these improvements, a new Hungarian translation was published in 2010, in one volume together with Ferenczi's correspondence with Georg Groddeck.

The letters in the present volume were translated from German into English by Beate Schumacher (psychoanalyst, member of the BPAS), who turned out to be a true successor to Joan Suttie in that she was able to find a way of translating not only the meaning, but also the affective charge of Ferenczi's words. Her attention to detail and style made her contribution to this volume even more valuable.

The first version of the introductory essay was translated from Hungarian into English by Mark Baczoni, and the final text was also reviewed by him.

We want to express our gratitude to Anna Kovács for her invaluable contribution to editing the texts and the notes. We are also thankful to Ildikó Kovács for her technical assistance.

In preparing the publication of this correspondence, we received support, assistance, and advice from various institutions and colleagues. First of all, we thank the Archives of the British Psychoanalytical Society for their extensive and enthusiastic support, and Judith Dupont (Paris) who gave us permission to publish Ferenczi's letters to Jones.

A research grant from the Hungarian National Research Fund (OTKA K 79146) made possible several trips by Ferenc Erős to London to work in the Archives. Special thanks are due to the recently closed Collegium Budapest, Institute for Advanced Studies, from whom Ferenc Erős received a fellowship during the academic year 2010–2011. Last, but not least, we thank Imago International and the Joir and Kato Weisz Foundation (London) for their generous support.

This volume could not have been realised without the enthusiastic help of our series editors, Peter Rudnytsky and Brett Kahr.

Ferenc Erős, Ken Robinson, and Judit Székács

ABOUT THE EDITORS

Ferenc Erős studied psychology and literature at the ELTE University in Budapest, and graduated in 1969. He obtained his PhD in 1986, and he has borne the title "Doctor of the Hungarian Academy of Sciences" (DSc) since 2002. Currently, he is Professor of Social Psychology at the Faculty of Humanities of the University of Pécs, where he has directed a doctoral programme in psychoanalytic studies since 1997. He also directs a social psychological research unit at the Institute of Cognitive Neuroscience and Psychology, at the Research Centre of Natural Sciences of the Hungarian Academy of Sciences in Budapest. In the academic year 2010–2011, he was a senior fellow at the Collegium Budapest, Institute for Advanced Studies. The focus of his present research areas include the social and cultural history of psychoanalysis in Central Europe, psychoanalytic theory and its application to social issues, and the problem of trauma and cultural memory. He edited the Hungarian translation of the Freud–Ferenczi correspondence, and, in his areas of research, is the author of several scientific books and articles in English, Hungarian, German, and French. He founded *Thalassa*, the journal of the Sándor Ferenczi Society in Budapest, which he edited from 1990–2010. At present, he edits *Imágó Budapest*, the journal of the Hungarian Imago Association.

Judit Szekacs-Weisz is a bilingual psychoanalyst and psychotherapist, a member of the British Psychoanalytical Society and the Group of Independent Psychoanalysts, and a training analyst of the Hungarian Psychoanalytical Society. Born and educated (mostly) in Budapest, she has absorbed the ideas and way of thinking of Ferenczi, the Balints, Hermann, and Rajka as integral parts of a "professional mother tongue". The experience of living and working in a totalitarian regime sensitised her to the social and individual aspects of trauma, identity formation, and strategies of survival. Szekacs-Weisz was a founding member of the Sándor Ferenczi Society, Budapest. In 1990, she moved to London, where, with a small group of psychoanalysts, therapists, artists, and social scientists, she founded Imago East West, and, later, the Multilingual Psychotherapy Centre (MLPC) to create a space where diverse experiences of living and changing context and language in different cultures can be explored and creative solutions found. She is the author of several articles, and co-editor of *Lost Childhood and the Language of Exile* (Freud Museum & Imago East West, 2004). Together with Tom Keve, she co-edited *Ferenczi and His World* and *Ferenczi for Our Time*, both published by Karnac Books, London, in 2012. Szekacs-Weisz is President of Imago International.

Ken Robinson is a psychoanalyst in private practice in Newcastle upon Tyne and the Honorary Archivist for the British Psychoanalytical Society. He is a training analyst for trainings in child, adolescent, and adult psychotherapy in the North of England and in Scotland. He lectures and teaches in the UK and Europe, and is especially interested in the developmental point of view, the nature of therapeutic action, and the history of psychoanalysis. His most recent publication is a brief history of the British Psychoanalytical Society.

SERIES EDITOR'S FOREWORD

Peter L. Rudnytsky

The history of psychoanalysis unfolds simultaneously on the plane of ideas and theories and as a gripping drama of human relationships. If the story of psychoanalysis as an intellectual discipline is recorded primarily in the works published by Freud and other authors during their lifetimes, for the subjective underside the most indispensable sources are the private letters that, for the most part, see the light of day only posthumously, if at all.

By virtue of his primacy in the external, public narrative, as well as the sheer fecundity of his genius, Freud is, likewise, the chief protagonist in the backstage epistolary intrigues of psychoanalysis. Almost all of his major correspondences have now been published in their entirety. But, for the true aficionado, there is an equal fascination in witnessing the sub-plots to the spectacle, where the supporting actors in Freud's cast step forward as leading men and women in their own right. Despite its fragmentary quality, and being disappointingly one-sided, the eminence of its interlocutors must give this volume a special place among the editions of psychoanalytic correspondences not involving Freud himself.

In Sándor Ferenczi and Ernest Jones, we have the two members of the first-generation inner circle who have exerted the greatest influence on posterity: Jones, above all, through his three-volume biography which played an integral role in shaping the image of Freud that prevailed for most of the twentieth century, and Ferenczi as the initially eclipsed pioneer whose work and reputation have undergone a rehabilitation in the past quarter century—in tandem with the loosening of the hold of Jones' "official" version of Freud's life and the history of psychoanalysis—to the point where Ferenczi is widely recognised as the indispensable precursor of a broad range of contemporary trends from relational psychoanalysis to self psychology. The fates of the two men are intertwined with particular intimacy by virtue of the fact that Ferenczi was Jones' analyst, and the letters presented here allow us to recapitulate in condensed form the entire history of their relationship.

As the volume opens on 8 April 1911, we find Ferenczi and Jones standing shoulder to shoulder as Freudian loyalists. Ferenczi derides the opponents of psychoanalysis as impelled not by intellectual disagreements, but by emotional insecurities: "It is no use to struggle or resist; its biggest enemies are those who suffer most from its revelations; Ziehen, Kräpelin and Oppenheim must have to dream psychoanalysis, given their rejection of it by day". Similarly, Adler "scotomises sexuality in a rather tendentious fashion", and Ferenczi cautions that others who do not "have a firm grasp of things" might join Adler and Stekel "in this 'reactionary' departure". On a personal note, Ferenczi thanks Jones for the "detailed and appreciative review of my work on suggestion", presumably referring—according to the editors—to the use made by Jones in "The action of suggestion in psychotherapy" (1911) of a section of Ferenczi's "Introjection and transference" (1909), although in 1912 Ferenczi published "Suggestion and psychoanalysis", and this paper might conceivably have been sent to Jones in manuscript a year earlier.

In his subsequent letter, written on 14 November 1911, Ferenczi remarks that "Freud is likely to be right . . . that a personal complex has played a role for me". The absence of the letter from Jones to which Ferenczi is replying again makes it difficult to ascertain his exact meaning. The editors direct our attention to Ferenczi's paper, "On the part played by homosexuality in the pathogenesis of paranoia" (1911), although the concern with impotence in the letter also points in the direction of "The analytic interpretation and treatment of psychical impotence" (1908). In any event, it was in July 1911 that

Ferenczi took into analysis Elma Pálos, the daughter of his married lover, Gizella Pálos, with whom Ferenczi had been having an affair since 1900, and he had by the end of the year fallen in love with Elma, causing an upheaval in his life. As I have argued elsewhere (Rudnytsky, 2013), even before his infatuation with Elma, Ferenczi not only must have recognised himself in Freud's paper, "A special type of choice of object made by men" (1910h), where Freud employed the term "Oedipus complex" for the first time, as well as in "The universal tendency to debasement in the sphere of love" (1912d), but also have served as one of the models on whom Freud based his theories in these papers on love. Thus, when Ferenczi states that Freud is correct in imputing to him a "personal complex", he seems to be acknowledging the presence of a subterranean biographical dimension in Freud's texts as well as in his own. With these circumstances in mind, it becomes impossible to read Ferenczi's twin avowals in this letter to Jones that "the infantile situation with regards to father and mother is like that of a jealous affair with a married woman, where the cuckolded husband is empathised with at the same time", and that "husbands are 'blind' when it comes to the wife's 'gentleman friend' . . . [b]ecause they are happy in this threesome and do not wish to change the situation", without viewing them as veiled commentaries on the infantile determinants of his own affair with Gizella Pálos and his ambivalent attitude toward her husband, Géza.

The solidarity between Ferenczi and Jones as Freudian loyalists is reflected in Ferenczi's repeated tendency to refer to the "enemies" of psychoanalysis, as he does again in his letters on 2 November 1912 and 25 October 1913. The former letter especially targets Stekel, while the latter, in which Ferenczi claims to have found "proof" of the existence of telepathy, takes aim at the paper delivered by Eugen Bleuler in May 1913 at the Congress of German Psychiatrists in Breslau, at which psychoanalysis suffered a resounding defeat at the hands of its opponents (see Borch-Jacobsen & Shamdasani, 2012; Falzeder & Burnham, 2007). Not surprisingly, as a counter-offensive was being mounted against Jung, Ferenczi writes to Jones on 8 November 1913, "After all, one will find true 'psychoanalysis' where Freud is himself".

Striking a lighter note are the inside jokes enlivening the correspondence. In his letter of 25 September 1913, which contains precocious reflections on the "death drive" inspired by Lou Salomé, Ferenczi takes exception to a "nonsensical, confused and malicious article" in the German-language newspaper *Pester Lloyd*, written by one Albert Ehrenstein, of whom Ferenczi says he has not heard but "whose name obviously does not oblige him in the slightest". This is a witticism playing on Stekel's 1911 paper, "The obligation of the name", since Ehrenstein means "honour stone" but Ferenczi believes he has acted dishonourably by demeaning psychoanalysis and, hence, not lived up to his name, while Ferenczi's jest about a patient in whom he has not "found a single prospective dream" alludes disparagingly to the 1912 paper by Jung's ally, Alphonse Maeder, "On the function of dreams", which is again criticised by Ferenczi on 16 December 1913.

Although it goes unmentioned until Ferenczi's letter of 20 July 1914, a turning point in their relationship came the preceding year, when Jones travelled to Budapest for twice-daily analysis with Ferenczi in June and July of 1913. In the background, as Ferenc Erős, Judit Szekacs-Weisz, and Ken Robinson note in their valuable introduction, is not only Ferenczi's imbroglio with Gizella and Elma, but also Jones' entanglement with his common-law wife, Loe Kann, and her maid, Lina. As he did with Elma Pálos, Freud took Loe Kann into analysis, thereby intervening directly in the love affairs of both disciples. Ironically, on 1 June 1914, Loe Kann, exhibiting an "obligation of the name", married the American poet Herbert Jones in Budapest, with Freud, Rank, and Ferenczi as witnesses. Yet again, therefore, Ferenczi's comment on 25 September 1913 that the analyst should abstain from giving "moral advice" so that "the question of 'permission' for extramarital intercourse becomes irrelevant" and the patient will "be able to make decisions about his personal relationships himself, but he also has to learn to take responsibility for them", possesses a subjective significance both for himself and for Jones, and, indeed, can be applied to all the early analysts who found themselves occupying one or another corner of an adulterous triangle.

Initially, Jones' extremely condensed analysis with Ferenczi led to a deepening of the friendship between the two men. Despite being five years Jones' senior and also in a position of authority as his analyst, Ferenczi writes on 16 March 1914 in a spirit of mutuality about his "neurasthenic insomnia" and "dilatoriness" in carrying out his plans for work. On 23 June 1914, Ferenczi signs off for the first time using the intimate German form *Du* instead of the formal *Sie*. To be sure, in his letters to Freud, Ferenczi permits himself to share confidences about his patient, remarking on 17 June 1913—in an extract quoted by the editors—that Jones' "excessive kindness works as a hindrance in the analysis; his dreams are full of mockery and scorn toward me" (Brabant, Falzeder, & Giampieri-Deutsch, 1993, p. 493). Uncannily, the dynamic of conscious subservience and unconscious resentment that Ferenczi diagnoses in Jones likewise obtains in his own relationship with Freud, with whom Ferenczi was in analysis on three occasions, for less than six weeks in total, in 1914 and 1916. (It is worth pausing to reflect on the brevity of the therapeutic experiences of both Jones and Ferenczi, as well as of other pioneers such as Eitingon and Rank, while still others—Abraham and, of course, Freud himself—created psychoanalysis without ever having entrusted themselves to anyone else for treatment.) Notwithstanding his recognition of Jones' ambivalence, the warmth of Ferenczi's feelings toward him is unmistakable when he informs Freud on 5 August 1913, four days after Jones had left Budapest, "I miss him *very much*. We have become intimate friends; I grew to love and treasure him; it was a pleasure to have such an intelligent, fine, and respectable pupil" (Brabant, Falzeder, & Giampieri-Deutsch, 1993, p. 503).

That the relationship between Ferenczi and Jones began so auspiciously renders the subsequent course of events all the more lamentable. A *leitmotif* is Ferenczi's effort to persuade Jones to resume his truncated analysis. In a letter symptomatically misdated 20 July 1913, while Jones was still in Budapest, but almost certainly written one year later, Ferenczi accepts an invitation to come to London, where he fears he will be a burden, but adds, "by way of recompense for all of this trouble, you must accept, at the very least, that while I am there we continue with the training analysis you began with me here. I am thinking of proper analytic sessions". Despite the apparent magnanimity of this gesture, it exerts pressure on Jones to accept Ferenczi's offer of additional analysis as a way of repaying him for the hospitality Ferenczi expected to receive in London, and, hence, coerces Jones into feeling a debt of gratitude to his analyst for bestowing the ostensibly free "gift" of his services.

The outbreak of the First World War prevented Ferenczi from travelling to England, and in the event he did not set foot there until 1927, on his way back from America, though he was elected to Honorary Membership in the British Psychoanalytical Society in 1920, six years after Jones had been accorded the same recognition by the Hungarian Psychoanalytical Association. The submerged tensions in their relationship came to the fore in 1923 following the meeting of the Committee in San Cristoforo, the first from which Freud was absent and which was overshadowed by the news of his cancer, where Jones had been taken to task for anti-Semitic comments directed against Rank, with whom he had been in conflict. As Ferenczi wrote on 7 October 1923, "I do not consider you an out-and-out neurotic either, but am firmly of the opinion that you are in need of analysis, not only because of your, as I believe, unconsciously motivated actions, but also because I must consider your previous analysis incomplete just on the grounds of my technique having been far less perfected at the time". Although Ferenczi attempts to soften the blow by blaming his own technique for the unsatisfactory result ten years earlier, he urges Jones to "start a proper analysis", appending the qualification, "How this might fit with the demands of your life I am, of course, unable to judge".

The first letter from Jones in this collection is dated 7 August 1924, a ten-month delayed response to Ferenczi's letter of 7 October 1923. In the interim, Ferenczi had reproached Jones for failing properly to credit him in his 1923 paper, "The nature of auto-suggestion", which revived Ferenczi's earlier resentment, masked by an expression of thanks, against Jones for having allegedly plagiarised him in "The action of suggestion in psychotherapy", although Ferenczi voices the hope, on 13 January 1924, that this controversy would not "mar our relationship forever, or even in the short term", and that the future would "offer us both opportunities to demonstrate good will and kindness". Notwithstanding the olive branch extended by Ferenczi, Jones' letter of 7 August 1924 shows him attempting to turn the tables and, for the first time, gaining the upper hand in their interactions. His weapon is Ferenczi's collaboration with Rank, now stigmatised as a heretic destined to go the way of Jung. As Jones needles Ferenczi in the guise of reassuring him, "No one identifies you with him in this respect, though it is a great puzzle to know how you came to write a book in common". With respect to his analysis, Jones professes to be eager to resume his role as patient: "I had, and still have, a strong desire to continue the analysis, chiefly because the most perfect attainable is the ideal we should all aim at in connection with psychoanalysis". But the insincerity of this avowal is exposed when Jones concludes by informing Ferenczi that, in view of his flourishing state of emotional health, he has nothing to gain from spending any additional time on the couch: "I can only console myself with the thought that anyone who is so happy in his love-life as I am and able to work satisfactorily cannot be in any urgent need of further analysis, and I am sure you would agree with this criterion".

The ensuing letters show Ferenczi back-pedalling while simultaneously seeking to repair the breach in their relationship. On 18 August 1924, he defends his joint work with Rank, *Developmental Aims of Psychoanalysis* (1924), saying that its flaws are mainly ones of "style and editing", but "overall" he does "stand by the views expressed there". By 29 May 1925, however, Ferenczi denounces Rank's technical innovations, of which reports had reached him from America, as "wholly mistaken", while Rank's theory of the birth trauma is discounted as nothing more than a "neurotic phantasy". He reaches out to Jones with the appeal, "I think it is time, now the scientific–political hatchet has been buried, we re-established our previously good personal relations". On the cusp of the transformative innovations of his final phase, Ferenczi modestly brings Jones up to date on his work, "In terms of theory, nothing essential is going on with me", although from his clinical practice he is "learning quite a bit, not just objectively, but about myself personally".

A minor point of disagreement between Ferenczi and Jones stemmed from Jones' distaste for Ferenczi's analysand, Marjorie Ellen Franklin, a psychiatrist and one of the founders of what became the Portman Clinic. Urging that Franklin deserved to be accepted as a member by the British Psychoanalytical Society, based on her more than two years of analysis with him, Ferenczi argues that despite "some personal difficulties in her character", her "capability and scientific knowledge are so valuable that we must be lenient". Appealing to the principle of charity, he makes the point that, like all analysts, "she needs the friendly attitude of her colleagues", for "who of us is quite free from character difficulties?"

The climactic moment in this correspondence comes in Ferenczi's letter of 6 January 1930. In response to a missing letter from Jones, in which he had evidently charged Ferenczi with ambivalence, Ferenczi opens by acknowledging harbouring critical feelings toward Jones, due in no small measure to the latter's tergiversations in the controversies over lay analysis: "The ambivalence of which you speak is undeniable, but the feeling is quite mutual. Your ambiguous behaviour with regard to the question of lay analysis (!) has contributed a great deal to the increase in negativity on my part". As one reads on, it emerges that Jones's accusation against Ferenczi had been prompted by the paper Ferenczi had contributed to the *Festschrift* in honour of Jones' fiftieth birthday, "The unwelcome child and his death-instinct" (1929), to which Jones must have taken exception. Now fully in the creative throes of his final period, Ferenczi states that he had been led to choose the topic of his paper by reading the short paper Jones had contributed to *his* fiftieth-birthday *Festbuch*, "Cold, illness and birth" (1923), the theme of which "then became associated with another one, which has been preoccupying me for some time and which belongs to a body of work yet to be published; I am referring to the life instinct and infantile trauma". Alluding to the psychoanalytic Congress held the previous summer in Oxford, Ferenczi proceeds to reflect on their reciprocal recriminations: "Against the charge that, unconsciously, I wanted to offend you, there is of course no defence. Only, you too would have to ask yourself whether your interpretation might not spring from that irritability we had many an opportunity to observe in Oxford.—Who might be the objective judge here? Not even Eitingon, I believe".

What is most striking about this exchange is that Jones and Ferenczi are analysing each other through reading each other's texts—or each other *as* texts. Jones interprets Ferenczi's paper, written to commemorate Jones' fiftieth birthday, and prompted by the paper Jones had written for Ferenczi's fiftieth birthday, as an expression of Ferenczi's ambivalence, while Ferenczi counters by imputing Jones' interpretation to his "irritability", and argues that allegations of unconscious motives are, by their very nature, irrefutable and double-edged, so that there can be no "objective judge" in such *ad hominem* disputes. Ferenczi drives home his conclusion, "Thus, I am left with no other option than to return, with all due respect, the compliment of my contribution being unconscious and therefore analysable (!)". Although the editors offer two possible glosses for Ferenczi's reference to "my contribution", I think it is clear from the context that he can mean only his contribution to Jones' *Festschrift*—that is, "The unwelcome child and his death-instinct"—that has been the bone of his contention with Jones throughout the letter.

Once this is understood, it becomes possible to interpret Ferenczi's compulsion to "return the compliment" to Jones not simply as a general caution against charging one's colleagues with motives that are "unconscious and therefore analysable", but as a critique directed specifically against Jones' paper written for Ferenczi's fiftieth-birthday *Festbuch*, "Cold, illness and birth", which had instigated Ferenczi's "ambivalent" response, and, thereby, set the avalanche in motion. "[S]eeing we are exchanging home truths", Ferenczi permits himself to expatiate, "I do not read your work with undivided pleasure either. If my papers are wild and fantastical, yours often give the impression of a kind of logical–sadistic violence, particularly since the, by the way, equally fantastical papers on child analysis appeared, I have not been enamoured with your English group at all."

Ferenczi's final statement registers his disenchantment with the "English school" forming around his erstwhile analysand, Melanie Klein, whose oversight in neglecting to inform him of her resignation from the Hungarian Psychoanalytic Society had elicited a protest on 12 June 1921. Ferenczi's distancing of himself from Klein prefigures the rift between the Kleinians in the British Psychoanalytical Society, with their "fantastical" version of object relations theory, and members of the Middle or Independent Group, represented pre-eminently by Winnicott, who hearken back to Ferenczi in their attention to the role of environmental factors in psychic life. Indeed, although Ferenczi continues to employ the term "death instinct" in his 1929 paper, the thesis he actually propounds concerning the "unwelcome child" is, in fact, incompatible with this dubious postulate of Freudian—and Kleinian—metapsychology. For Ferenczi's contention is that acutely self-destructive patients must have had their desire to live weakened as children by "conscious or unconscious signs of aversion or impatience on the part of the mother" and have been "received in a harsh and unloving way" (pp. 104–105). Ferenczi closely anticipates Winnicott in stressing that the maturational processes intrinsic to "the organs and other functions", both before and after birth, will unfold in unimpeded fashion "only under the particularly favourable conditions of germinal and infantile protection provided by the environment" (p. 105). Although Ferenczi acknowledges that individuals "who develop a precocious aversion to life" resemble those who, "in Freud's grouping, suffer from an inherited weakness in their capacity for life"—that is, from a surplus of the death instinct—he immediately adds that there is "the difference that in all our cases the innateness of the sickly tendency is deceptive and not genuine, owing to the early incidence of the trauma" (p. 106). Thus, by the time Ferenczi has concluded his discourse, he is not talking about innate causes of self-destructiveness at all, but rather about the ways that, as he puts it in his letter to Jones, the "life instinct" can be assaulted and maimed by the effects of "infantile trauma".

The principal point of Jones' 1923 paper, by contrast, is to show that the superstitious belief that "'cold air causes disease'" goes back to "the sensation of cold air" experienced by the infant "on being expelled from paradise" at birth, and "the dominant impression thus received on the threshold of life remains for ever after connected with the ideas of discomfort, insecurity, danger, or even bodily harm" (p. 324). Ironically, one year before the publication of Rank's *The Trauma of Birth*, which Jones was to denounce as a retreat from the Oedipus complex, Jones credits Ferenczi with providing "our first proper appreciation of the psychical significance that the act of birth must have for the infant" (p. 324). But, in Jones' account, the sensation of coldness that renders birth distressing to the neonate is purely physiological and has nothing to do with the debilitating effects of maternal rejection highlighted by Ferenczi. Beneath the surface of cordiality in their respective fiftieth-birthday tributes, in which each man begins by expressing his indebtedness to the other's work, therefore, Jones is espousing a non-relational, and Ferenczi a relational, conception of human experience, and, hence, two fundamentally divergent philosophies of psychoanalysis.

The illumination provided by Ferenczi's letter of 6 January 1930 reveals depths of meaning in Jones' "Cold, illness and birth" and Ferenczi's "The unwelcome child and his death-instinct" that would otherwise be difficult to discern and it brings into prominence the intersubjective dialogue taking place in and through the two papers. Even more than that, a juxtaposition of Ferenczi's private letter and the two published texts illustrates the overarching principle that the history of psychoanalysis unfolds at once on the plane of contested ideas and theories and as a drama of fragile and volatile human relationships.

With Ferenczi's retort that, if his own writings can be accused of being "wild and fantastical", then Jones' display "logical–sadistic violence", we reach the nadir of the personal story that began with such promise. The two majors in Freud's army, formerly united against all enemies, end by falling out with one another, as Jones remained loyal to the general while Ferenczi sought to give birth to what we can now recognise as an Independent or relational tradition of psychoanalysis. The tragic epilogue is found in Jones' biography of Freud, where he calumnies Ferenczi (as well as Rank) for having, "toward the end of his life, developed psychotic manifestations that revealed themselves in, among other ways, a turning away from Freud and his doctrines" (1957, p. 45; see Bonomi, 1999)—as though agreement with Freud were a criterion of mental health—a narrative that dominated psychoanalytic history for decades, until the "Ferenczi renaissance" inaugurated by the publication of the *Clinical Diary* in 1985.

Still, we find Jones and Ferenczi trying to valiantly to rekindle the spark of friendship and comity that prevailed in their halcyon days. Responding on 1 April 1931 to a lost letter from Jones, even as he warmed to the idea of becoming president of the International Psychoanalytic Association (though he was soon to conclude that he could not accept this honour in view of his estrangement from Freud), Ferenczi took pleasure in the sensation that "this wave of bad feeling has ebbed for both of us", and proposed that each of them draw from their conflict the still-timely lesson that "especially we psychoanalysts (!) should be more careful about not letting scientific–technical differences degenerate into personal ones than we have been hitherto".

In the last lines of his final communication, on 22 March 1933, exactly one month before his death, Ferenczi informs Jones that the roses the latter had sent him as a gift "seem to have endured the winter rather nicely", and expresses the hope that they "will often remind me of both you and your beautiful country-place". The editors helpfully include an extract from Ferenczi's final entry in his *Clinical Diary*, dated 2 October 1932, in which he states he was "pleasantly touched" by Jones' roses and some "personally friendly lines" in an accompanying letter that has not been preserved. In the same entry, Ferenczi goes on to write,

> Interestingly, the affair with brother J. offers me an opportunity (concurrently with the Freudian controversy) to have it out with J.—that is, to acknowledge the *reality* (hopelessness) in this direction also, and to make it known to the other party. Open antipathy instead of feigned amicability. (Dupont, 1985, p. 213)

In her note glossing Ferenczi's allusion to "brother J.", Judith Dupont asserts, "undoubtedly this refers" to his elder brother "Jakab, called

Joseph, born on 14 July 1869" (p. 215). But might not "brother J." be rather Ferenczi's younger brother in the psychoanalytic movement, and the entire paragraph express his resolution once and for all "to have it out with" Jones, even if accepting the hopeless reality of the situation entails placing their relationship on a footing of "open antipathy instead of feigned amicability"? Be that as it may, let us pause to smell the roses, and allow their perfume to linger as we contemplate this book of letters between Sándor Ferenczi and Ernest Jones.

References

Bonomi, C. (1999). Flight into sanity: Jones's allegation of Ferenczi's mental deterioration reconsidered. *International Journal of Psychoanalysis, 80*: 507–542.

Borch-Jacobsen, M., & Shamdasani, S. (2012). *The Freud Files: An Inquiry into the History of Psychoanalysis*. Cambridge: Cambridge University Press.

Brabant, E., Falzader, E., & Giampieri-Deutsch, P. (Eds.) (1993). *The Correspondence of Sigmund Freud and Sándor Ferenczi. Volume 1, 1908–1914*, P. T. Hoffer (Trans.). Cambridge, MA: Harvard University Press.

Dupont, J. (Ed.) (1985). *The Clinical Diary of Sándor Ferenczi*, M. Balint & N. Zarday Jackson (Trans.). Cambridge, MA: Harvard University Press, 1988.

Falzeder, E. M., & Burnham, J. C. (2007). A perfectly staged 'concerted action' against psychoanalysis: the 1913 congress of German psychiatrists. *International Journal of Psychoanalysis*, 88: 1223–1244.

Ferenczi, S. (1929). The unwelcome child and his death-instinct. In: *Final Contributions to the Problems and Methods of Psychoanalysis* (pp. 102–107), M. Balint (Ed.), E. Mosbacher et al. (Trans.) New York: Brunner/Mazel, 1980.

Jones, E. (1923). Cold, illness and birth. In: *Papers on Psychoanalysis* (pp. 320–324). Boston, MA: Beacon Press, 1961.

Jones, E. (1957). *The Life and Work of Sigmund Freud, Vol. 3, The Last Phase, 1919–1939*. New York: Basic Books.

Rudnytsky, P. L. (2013). Freud, Ferenczi, and *Rosmersholm*: incestuous triangles and analytic thirds. *American Journal of Psychoanalysis*, in press.

ABBREVIATIONS

BPAS Archives	Archives of the British Psychoanalytical Society, London
Bul Int Psychoanal Assn	*Bulletin of the International Psychoanalytical Association*
Die Rundbriefe, 1, 2, 3, 4	The circular letters of the "Secret Committee" *Volume 1. 1913–1920; Volume 2: 1921; Volume 3: 1922; Volume 4: 1923–1927* (Wittenberger & Tögel, 1999–2006)
Ferenczi–Groddeck	*The Sándor Ferenczi & Georg Groddeck Correspondence* (Fortune, 2002)
Freud–Abraham	*Sigmund Freud & Karl Abraham Correspondence* (Falzeder, 2002)
Freud–Eitingon, 1, 2	*Sigmund Freud und Max Eitingon: Briefwechsel 1906–1939* (Sigmund Freud & Max Eitingon: Correspondence 1906–1939) (2 Volumes) (Schröter, 2004)
Freud–Ferenczi, 1	*The Correspondence of Sigmund Freud and Sándor Ferenczi, Volume 1, 1908–1914* (Falzeder & Brabant, 1994)

Freud–Ferenczi, 2	*The Correspondence of Sigmund Freud and Sándor Ferenczi, Volume 2, 1914–1919* (Falzeder & Brabant, 1996)
Freud–Ferenczi, 3	*The Correspondence of Sigmund Freud and Sándor Ferenczi, Volume 3, 1920–1933.* (Falzeder & Brabant, 2000)
Freud–Jones	*The Complete Correspondence of Sigmund Freud and Ernest Jones (1908–1939)* (Paskaukas, 1993)
Freud–Jung	*The Freud–Jung Letters: The Correspondence between Sigmund Freud and C. G. Jung* (McGuire, 1994)
Imago	*Imago. Zeitschrift für Anwendung der Psychoanalyse auf die Geisteswissenschaften*
IPA	International Psychoanalytical Association
Jahrbuch	*Jahrbuch für psychoanalytische und psychopathologische Forschungen*
Jones, 2, 3	*The Life and Work of Sigmund Freud, Volume 2: Years of Maturity 1901–1919* and *The Life and Work of Sigmund Freud, Volume 3: The Last Phase 1919–1939* (Jones, 1955 & 1957)
Journal	*The International Journal of Psychoanalysis* London
Minutes, 4	*Minutes of the Vienna Psychoanalytic Society, Volume 4: 1912–1918.* (Nunberg & Federn, 1974)
(Ψα)	*Psychoanalysis*
S.E.	*The Standard Edition of the Complete Psychological Works of Sigmund Freud, Volumes 1–24.*
Verlag	Internationaler Psychoanalytischer Verlag
Zeitschrift	*Internationale Zeitschrift für (ärtzliche) Psychoanalyse.* Leipzig, Vienna, Zürich
Zentralblatt	*Zentralblatt für Psychoanalyse. Medizinische Monatsschrift für Seelenkunde*

Introduction

Documents, as well as people, have their own stories. This is particularly true of the letters published in this volume. They speak to us of the past; they are fragments of cultural history, records of their age. They report facts, give us knowledge, and, at the same time, afford us an insight into relationships and emotional reactions that bring new life to events, even if they are already well known. They command our respect and bring out the researcher's innate thirst for discovery.

Letters stored in archives are mostly accessible to the public; none the less, it does happen from time to time that they hide for years – perhaps decades, sometimes – in a drawer, or at the bottom of a file. That is, in fact, more or less what happened to the majority of the exchange of letters between Sándor Ferenczi and Ernest Jones, published in the following pages. They lay low – some for eighty years – waiting for someone to take them in hand once more, among the files at the archives of the British Psychoanalytical Society. And there they might have remained for a good time to come, had we not had the chance to organise the second International Ferenczi Conference under the title of "CONFERENCZI (Hungarian Psychoanalytical Ideas Revisited)" in London in 2004. It was at this event that Pearl King, celebrated figure of the Independent Group and dedicated director of the Archives for several decades, pointed us in their direction.

A few weeks after the conference these letters found themselves once more in the light of day, on the reading tables of the archive, and we started the research that led us to the letters we present here. Besides the correspondence between Sándor Ferenczi and Ernest Jones, the Archives hold several letters between Ferenczi and another of his British analysands, John Rickman (BPAS Archives, P03-C-A-02 ; P04-C-C-04).

Ferenczi in Britain during his lifetime

Ferenczi's links to British psychoanalysis are manifold. Having been the analyst of Ernest Jones before the First World War and then analyst to several other figures in the contemporary British world of psychoanalysis after the war, Ferenczi was well known and well respected in London during his own lifetime, from the early 1920s onwards. In 1920, the British Society elected him—along with Rank—to Honorary Membership.

The first of Ferenczi's papers to appear in English was his "The psycho-analysis of suggestion and hypnosis" in 1912 (Ferenczi, 1912[94]). After that, the English-speaking world had to wait until Ernest Jones had completed his task of translating the first collection of Ferenczi's papers into English; *Contributions to Psycho-Analysis* appeared in America in 1916. After the war, with the founding of both the *International Journal* and the *British Journal of Medical Psychology* in 1920, his papers could appear in translation soon after they were published in German (and, in most cases, simultaneously in Hungarian). A future analysand, John Rickman, abstracted "Zur Psychoanalyse der paralytischen Geistesstörung [Psychoanalysis and the psychic disorders of general paresis]" by Ferenczi and Hollós at length in the *British Journal of Medical Psychology* (Rickman, 1925); he also oversaw and contributed to the second collection of papers in English, *Further Contributions to the Theory and Technique of Psycho-Analysis,* published a year later (Ferenczi, 1926[276]). Most of the translation for this second volume was by Jane Suttie, who had volunteered her services to Jones as a translator. She, with her husband Ian, became a major disseminator of Ferenczi's ideas. As she recognised, Ferenczi's personality is felt even through the written text. She was taken by Ferenczi's passion in expressing his ideas, writing to Jones,

> [H]e is rather a quaint creature from a translator's point of view. I confess myself helpless before his enthusiasm for inverted commas, capitals, brackets etc and found it the simplest thing just to keep meekly to his way of it. You can always blue pencil as you choose, but there is such a really Ferenczi atmosphere about his typographical eccentricities – especially his use of dashes – (!), that I succumbed after a very few struggles and perpetuated them faithfully.
>
> I really hope I have got most of his sometimes curiously convoluted sentences into fairly lucid English without losing touch with the original. (6th August 1921, Glasgow) (BPAS Archives, PO4-C-E-15)

Despite his relationship with Jones, it was some years before Ferenczi journeyed to England. He had arranged to visit and stay with Jones in the summer of 1914, but the outbreak of war put paid to his plans. Almost a decade later, in 1923, he planned to attend the International Congress of Psychology in Oxford in July, but then decided not to, probably because he did not want to interrupt his work on *Thalassa*. When he finally did visit in 1927, it was with his wife, Gizella, on their way back to Hungary after a stay of several months in the USA. They landed in Southampton and spent a few days packed with visits and engagements.

By the time of Ferenczi's visit, he had seven analysands in the British Society: Jones, Klein, Estelle Cole, David Eder, Ethilda Budgett-Meakin Herford, William Inman, and Marjorie Franklin. John Rickman did not enter analysis with him until 1928, but he was already interested in Ferenczi's work and in touch with him. All these figures wanted to have their fair share of Ferenczi's time and found it difficult to agree on a schedule. Steady and faithful Rickman thought that he had "been appointed a sort of majordomo" (letter to W. S. Inman, 13 May 1927), but Inman believed that the arrangements were in his hands, prompting Rickman to apologise that he had not wanted to monopolise Ferenczi (letters between Inman and Rickman, 15 and 16 May 1927, BPAS Archives, P03-C-B-03). By the time that David Eder and Estelle Cole sought to ensure their place in his timetable, Rickman had handed over arrangements to Inman and was confused about their details (letters between Eder and Rickman and Cole and

Rickman, 27 May 1927, BPAS Archives, P03-C-B-01). In between meeting socially with his analysands and colleagues, Ferenczi addressed the Medical and Educational Sections of the British Psychological Society on the 13th of June, on "The adaptation of the family to the child" (Ferenczi, 1928[281]), and the British Psychoanalytical Society on the 15 June, reporting on his "Instructional activities in America in 1926 to 1927". At the British Psychological Society, both Ernest Jones and Melanie Klein took part in the discussion of Ferenczi's paper and he replied particularly to their remarks. Two years later, Ferenczi returned to participate in the International Congress of Psychoanalysis in Oxford.

It is difficult to assess the influence that Ferenczi's British analysands had within the British psychoanalytic establishment in the transmission of his ideas. Jones and Rickman (before he had first-hand experience on Ferenczi's couch) played a major part in making his writings available in English, but, during Ferenczi's lifetime, only Jones, Klein, and Rickman were active within the training set up on the Eitingon model. Eder would have liked to have been, but it seems that he was blocked by Jones, who considered him a rival. Of course, Ferenczi is an important part of Jones' range of references in his own papers, but he was ambivalent about Ferenczi's flexibility in thinking about technique, especially after the publication of *Entwicklungsziele der Psychoanalyse: Zur Wechselbeziehung von Theorie und Praxis* [*The Development of Psychoanalysis*] in 1924 (Ferenczi & Rank, 1924). When, in the same year, Jones edited a collection of papers by members of the Society, *Social Aspects of Psycho-Analysis* (Jones, 1924c), he omitted Ferenczi's work from the list of "trustworthy presentations" of psychoanalysis at the end of the book, although he would include Ferenczi in the bibliography of his brief *Psycho-Analysis* in 1928 (Jones, 1928). Turning to Klein, Ferenczi himself was concerned during and after his visit to London in 1927 about the "prominent influence" (*Freud–Ferenczi, 3*, p. 313) that she was having on Jones and the British Society. In the ferment between Anna Freud and Klein from 1927 onwards, he pinned his colours to the former's mast. It is unclear to what extent candidates and colleagues might have felt Ferenczi's influence through Klein's own work, because she was so intensely engaged in building her own system. Rickman, however, recognised the continuity between their work, both in her extension into child analysis of Ferenczi's grasp of "the full implications of the transference situation" as a "here and now" phenomenon that offers "insight into . . . the mother–child relationship", as well as later developmental history, and in her interest in the magical beliefs of civilised children, which stemmed from Ferenczi's research into "The development of the sense of reality" (Rickman, 1933). It is likely that Rickman conveyed this continuity through his own work. Rickman's writings were deeply influenced by Ferenczi, even before his analysis. Clinically, he took on board Ferenczi's extension of Freud's practice with respect to transference, emphasising its "here-and-now" aspect (though he was also aware that, strictly speaking, transference neurosis was a here-and-now phenomenon for Freud, too). It is probable that Rickman chose Ferenczi as his second analyst because he needed to sort out in himself an early trauma that he felt Ferenczi would be more able to help him reach (King, 2003).

Estelle Cole was interested in technique (Cole, 1922) and went to Ferenczi "to learn", in Ferenczi's own words, "'active technique' from [him], but instead of that had to experience a piece of normal analysis on her own person" (*Freud–Ferenczi, 3*: p. 85). Among the remainder of Ferenczi's British analysands, Eder and Franklin's interest in the impact of the environment, and, in Franklin's case, "what environmental modifications, if any, might be helpful to an analysis", might have been influenced, or at least furthered, by their work with Ferenczi (Franklin, 1933, p. 107). Cole, Eder, and Herford were interested in the infantile mind, though Cole perhaps drew more on Adler than Ferenczi (Cole, 1928). The title of Herford's paper "The infantile mind and its relations to social problems and mental hygiene" (1928) could just as easily have been the title of a paper by Eder. From descriptions of Eder as an analyst, he seems to have been influenced in his own practice by his analyst's technical modifications (Thomson, 2011). If he was, this might have counted against him when it came to his wish to join the Training Committee. And Inman shared his concern with psychosomatic illness and symptoms with Herford (Payne, 1957). He was especially interested in ophthalmology, which he discussed with Ferenczi (Inman, 1958).

When we turn to Ferenczi's influence during his lifetime within the British Society more generally, we might expect to see the indigenous British interest in education, child development, and child analysis creating curiosity about Ferenczi's work, especially since his most influential paper in Britain was "Stages in the development of the sense of reality" (Ferenczi, 1913[111]). But this does not seem to have happened. The collection of papers designed to show off the Society's interest in children, edited by Ferenczi's ambassador, John Rickman, in 1936, *On the Bringing Up of Children*, does not contain a single reference to Ferenczi. Those contributing to the earlier Symposium on Child Analysis in the British Society in 1927 were similarly silent on the relevance of Ferenczi's work, except for Edward Glover. In both cases, it seems that Ferenczi was eclipsed by the prevailing enthusiasm for Klein's work; it is significant that there is also no reference to Abraham.

There were, however, British analysts who were not analysed by Ferenczi but who were more than usually influenced by his work. One was John Bowlby, who is discussed below. Winnicott is another, but here the influence is diffuse and difficult to characterise, not least because, as Enid Balint reported, he "openly said that he didn't want to read Ferenczi . . . because he wanted to think it out for himself. So he didn't read" (Rudnytsky, 2000, p. 19). A less obvious example is Karin Stephen, who interrupted her training in 1927 to travel to America where she met not only Ferenczi's analysand Izette de Forest Lord, but also Ferenczi himself, attending some of his seminars and enjoying the discussion "with great mutual satisfaction" (letters to her mother, 26 February and 27 March, 1927, in private hands). During her stay, Stephen had analysis with Clara Thompson, who would later move to Budapest for analysis with Ferenczi at the suggestion of Harry Stack Sullivan, becoming Ferenczi's major American follower. Although she does not refer to Ferenczi explicitly (she characteristically carries her learning lightly), her papers, especially "Introjection and projection: guilt and rage" (Stephen, 1934) and "Aggression in early childhood" (Stephen, 1939) show clear kinship with Ferenczi's thinking. Karin Stephen became a training analyst and, according to Marion Milner's obituary, "her quick grasp of any intellectual problem was a delight and an inspiration" for younger colleagues who met her (Milner, 1954, p. 433; see also Bradley, 2002, p. 229). Stephen's first analyst had been James Glover. When he died, she transferred to his brother Edward, and then to Sylvia Payne as her training analyst. Edward Glover, one of the finest minds in the British Society in his time, was, aside from Rickman, perhaps the analyst most influential in keeping Ferenczi's ideas fresh in the minds of his colleagues. Glover was very active within and without the Society. It was he who, in 1924, presented an abstract of *Entwicklungsziele der Psychoanalyse: Zur Wechselbeziehung von Theorie und Praxis* at a Scientific Meeting of the Society. In the same year, he published an essay, "'Active therapy' and psycho-analysis—a critical review" in which he contextualises and sets out at length the development of Ferenczi's ideas, adding an appendix on Ferenczi and Rank's book (Glover, 1924). This and his other engagements with Ferenczi's theoretical and clinical thinking, like his brilliant lectures on technique to candidates in 1927 (Glover, 1927–1928), are remarkable for their even-handed and respectful approach at a time when some, like Jones, tended to a knee-jerk negative suspicion or, as Glover puts it, "temporised in the hope of getting some authoritative guidance from Freud himself" (Glover, 1927, p. 419). Glover viewed Ferenczi's "name . . . [as] a byword for clinical sagacity, imaginative insight and hardiness of speculation" (Glover, 1927, p. 417). Theoretically, he found Ferenczi's conceptualisation of the development of a sense of reality fundamental to understanding perversions, delinquency, and criminality; it is interesting to note that several of the early members of the Institute for the Study and Treatment of Delinquency, which saw its first patient in 1933, were influenced, or analysed, by Ferenczi: David Eder, Marjorie Franklin, Ethilda Herford, Karin Stephen, and Glover himself.

Beyond the Society, the medical press regularly reported on Ferenczi's work. His work must have been known in German before it was translated into English because, as early as 1913, an anonymous reviewer in the *British Medical Journal* wrote that Ferenczi "has made many converts by his work on "Lélekelemzés (The analysis of the soul)" (12 June, 1913). There was, then, a foundation on which others who were not analysts might be drawn to Ferenczi, and not just from the medical world. In 1923, Ferenczi provided a foreword to Thomas Kenrick Slade's *Our Phantastic Emotions* (Slade, 1923). Slade, a psychologist, had enlisted the help of Ernest Jones to read his manuscript. But the most significant figure of this group was Ian Suttie, who, as husband to one of Ferenczi's translators, was well placed to know his work. Suttie was one of a like-minded group working at the Tavistock, which included J. A. Hadfield and John Bowlby. Suttie's *The Origins of Love and Hate* (1935), for which Hadfield provided an introduction, champions the importance of primary attachment against Freud's instinct theory. He writes,

> 'Instead of an armament of instincts, latent or otherwise, the child is born with a simple attachment-to-mother who is the sole source of food and protection . . . the need for a mother is primarily presented to the child mind as a need for company and as a discomfort in isolation.' Inevitably, therefore, there is anxiety at separation and a dread of loneliness: '. . . differences in handling, in the responsiveness of nurses and mothers, may produce great differences in the child's first impressions and reactions, and hence upon [his] whole future development . . .' (quoted in Bowlby, 1988, p. xvii)

This extract is taken from Bowlby's introduction to the 1988 reissue of Suttie's book, commenting on, and quoting from, it. Bowlby is paying tribute to its impact on his own work. Influenced directly by Ferenczi's emphasis on primary relatedness and "the role of real life events", as well as by Ferenczi's colleague Imre Hermann, who was already interested in ethology in relation to the infant's "clinging attitude", he was also indirectly influenced through Suttie (Bacciagaluppi, 1994, p. 97; Hermann, 1976[1935]). For Suttie, it follows that "the cure would then appear to be *restoration of that social confidence which is the basis of interest and the removal of the privation-anxiety which is the main disturber of the sex appetite*". "I fully accept," he writes, "Ferenczi's dictum 'The physician's love heals the patient'" (Suttie, 1988, p. 178). Gabriele Cassullo has recently argued that

> Suttie represented the very prototype of the Independent analyst, combining as he did an in-depth knowledge of, and interest in, Freudian theory with a 'structure of feeling' firmly grounded at once in British psychology and psychiatry and the Hungarian psychoanalytic tradition shaped by Ferenczi's legacy. (Cassullo, 2010, p. 18)

It is significant that the technical aspects of Ferenczi's later work made themselves felt most clearly outside, rather than inside, the British Society, which was still presided over by Jones as President. Of course, it was different after the arrival of the Bálints.

The Ferenczi–Jones correspondence as historical and personal document

The Ferenczi–Jones correspondence is an important document of the early history of psychoanalysis. It might cast new light on familiar events and developments we know from other sources, such as the Freud–Ferenczi and the Freud–Jones correspondence, the circular letters of the "Secret Committee" (*Rundbriefe*), and also from their various publications. The Ferenczi–Jones correspondence is not as comprehensive and all-embracing as the latter correspondences. At the same time, it spans more than two decades, and most of the relevant issues of the psychoanalytic movement during these two decades are reflected in them: Freud's relation to Wilhelm Stekel, Alfred Adler, and Carl Gustav Jung, the First World War, the debates of the 1920s regarding the theoretical and technical ideas and innovations of Otto Rank and Ferenczi, problems of group leadership, structure, finding a centre for the psychoanalytical movement, issues related to telepathy and lay analysis, etc.

Probably the most interesting aspect of these documents is how they allow us to look into an extraordinary relationship developing between these two important figures in the history of early psychoanalysis. Different capacities and personality traits, conflicts in their private lives, professional interests, theoretical disagreements, and – last but not least – group dynamics within the psychoanalytical movement all affected Ferenczi and Jones' ambivalent, sometimes fiercely undulating, relationship. Their relationship could hardly be termed harmonious; it was not devoid of rivalry and jealousy, sometimes of hidden passion, and even outright hostility. Nevertheless, friendship, sympathy, collegiality, and readiness for co-operation were just as important for Ferenczi and Jones as rivalry, mistrust, and suspicion.

Reading these letters, professional correspondence, and other documents of the pioneering years, one cannot help being drawn into the pictures of a not-so-unfamiliar but mostly forgotten past. The linkages cover the whole territory of human existence and reach far and deep.

Having a taste of the emotional atmosphere and socio-cultural background of our history adds a special flavour to rediscovering our professional past. Bringing it alive not only for psychoanalysts and psychotherapists, but for historians and other social scientists interested in the history of psychoanalysis, the Ferenczi–Jones correspondence can open up passages that help decode various aspects of the experience preserved in these documentary memories of former generations.

These letters belong to the "private", personal history of psychoanalysis. However, this body of correspondence also constitutes a significant part of the history of the movement as a whole, which, to a very large degree, rests on shared traditions and experience, and the tight – sometimes impenetrable – network of the members of these communities, their patients, and others who entered their orbit. The correspondence of Ferenczi and Jones allows us to build up a far more nuanced picture of the relationship of the two and of the complicated network system and group dynamics of which both were part.

The corpus of the correspondence comprises altogether thirty-seven letters and six postcards. Most of the letters are from Ferenczi to Jones; however, the collection also contains copies of three typed letters written by Jones to Ferenczi. According to our present knowledge, the rest of Jones' letters addressed to Ferenczi did not survive. Most of Ferenczi's letters are handwritten and are in German, a language Jones knew well. He, on the other hand, replied in English, the language he used in the *Rundbriefe* and elsewhere in his correspondence.

In his letters, Ferenczi addresses Jones as "Dear Jones", "Lieber Freund", and "Lieber Ernest" alternately. When writing in German, he initially used the formal, polite form of address (German *Sie*); however, after his letter dated 23 June 1914, he began using the informal form (*Du*).

First encounters

In this introduction we have to limit ourselves to highlighting just a few morsels of the relationship between Ferenczi and Jones that can be seen developing throughout this correspondence.

Ferenczi and Jones first met on the 27th April 1908, at the "First Congress of Freudian Psychiatry", held in Salzburg. After the congress, Jones—in the company of Abraham Brill—paid a visit to Budapest (*Freud–Ferenczi, 1*, p. 9). More than a year later, in the September of 1909, they met again, this time in America, at Clark University in Worcester, where Freud held his famous "five lectures". Their correspondence began one year later, in 1911.

Ferenczi first mentions on the 4th April 1911, in a letter to Freud (*Freud–Ferenczi, 1*, p. 266), that he has received a letter from Jones, who was in Canada as the neurologist of the University of Toronto. Jones, at this time, was very active in encouraging the spread of psychoanalysis in North America. It was clearly as a reply to this letter that Ferenczi's first letter to Jones was written four days later, thanking Jones for being so complimentary about his work on suggestion. He praises Jones' efforts in America on psychoanalysis's behalf, adding that

> ... psychoanalysis, once it is let loose, is like energy, it cannot be destroyed. It doesn't leave people in peace until they pursue it to the end. It's no use protesting or resisting; its biggest enemies are those who suffer most from the new revelations. Ziehen, Kraepelin and Oppenheim must dream about psychoanalysis while refuting it by day. (1F, p. 3)

At the end of his letter, Ferenczi expresses the hope that this would be "the beginning of a correspondence" (1F).

Their correspondence continued in this friendly tone, debating such issues as the significance of homosexuality, alcoholism, anxiety, and jealousy. In his letter of the 12th February 1912, Ferenczi joyfully informs Jones that Wilhelm Stekel, whom he now considers an enemy, has left the Association, adding that "[T]he Viennese are happy about Stekel's resignation – Prof. Freud is delighted with it" (3F, p. 12).

Jones in analysis with Ferenczi

Jones returned to Europe from Canada in May 1912 for a few months, and then permanently a year later. He had had a number of difficult experiences in his private life with his then partner, Loe Kann, who was struggling with her drug addiction; at the same time, he had got into professional difficulties owing to an accusation of abuse against him by a female patient,[1] never fully explained. At Jones' request, Freud undertook Loe's analysis, which continued when, a year later, in June and July of 1913, Jones stayed in Budapest in order to undertake two hours of training analysis a day with Ferenczi. Their analyses gave them both a chance to form a more complete picture of each other's character and, at the same time, to deepen their friendship. As we can read in the following excerpts from their letters, they did not hesitate to bring their impressions of each other and the analysis to Freud's attention:

Ferenczi on Jones (7 June 1913)

I think the analysis with Jones will work. At present he is interpreting too much and is producing only old material that is already known to him; he has already brought the (positive) transference along into the treatment. He is very keen on honesty (I know that from comparing what he has already said with what I know about him). (*Freud–Ferenczi, 1*, p. 490)

Ferenczi on Jones (17 June 1913)

Jones is very pleasant as a friend and colleague. His excessive kindness works as a hindrance in the analysis; his dreams are full of mockery and scorn toward me, which he has to admit, without being able really to believe in these hidden characteristics of his. . . . I now find Jones in some respects scientifically much more valuable to us than before our analytic acquaintance with him. But he is inhibited in production by his excess of kindness; he forbids himself any independence, which then avenges itself by means of an inclination toward intrigue and secret triumphs, treachery. (*Freud–Ferenczi, 1*, p. 493)

Jones on Ferenczi (17 June 1913)

I am doing my best in the analysis and think it is going on satisfactorily. Ferenczi discovers in me very strong aggressive tendencies which I have reacted to by too much suppression and submissiveness, and which revenge themselves in various impulsive tendencies. (*Freud–Jones*, p. 204).

Ferenczi on Jones (23 June and July 7 1913)

Jones is my best and dearest patient; he is competent, clever, obedient, and a really dependable friend at the same time; I think we will be able to build on him.

[H]e is not only good and sensitive but also a very clever person, whose company stimulates one to one's best thoughts. (*Freud–Ferenczi, 1*, p. 494 and p. 498)

Jones on Ferenczi (22 July 1913)

[The analysis] has without doubt been successful in making me face more clearly various character traits and dangerous tendencies, and I

> trust that it will prove its value also when it comes to be tested in actual life. I cannot praise Ferenczi too highly for his skill and tact throughout, and he has also succeeded in making it congruous with the analysis to be very kind . . . so that on the whole I have had a very enjoyable time in Budapest. (*Freud–Jones*, p. 213)

Ferenczi on Jones (26 July 1913)

> Jones is working diligently; I hope the analysis will be useful to him in every respect; he was still not able to emancipate himself completely from his latent tendencies (although he is thinking very optimistically about it). (*Freud–Ferenczi, 1*, p. 501)

Ferenczi on Jones (5 August 1913)

> Jones left me four days ago. I miss him very much. We have become intimate friends; I grew to love and treasure him; it was a pleasure to have such an intelligent, fine, and respectable pupil. His convictions were more securely based, his self-reliance increased, and probably also his courage to be somewhat more original. Let us hope he will succeed in mastering his neurotic tendencies from now on – but I will not venture to make a definite prognosis on this. (*Freud–Ferenczi, 1*, p. 502)

It is quite obvious here how Ferenczi viewed Jones' analysis with great expectations, albeit he also voices some doubts regarding Jones's future professional and personal development. The two years preceding the outbreak of the First World War were the period of the "soap opera" of (to adapt Michael Bálint's phrase) "couch calamities". Elma was in analysis first with Ferenczi, who later sent her to Freud hoping that their relationship dilemmas could be solved there. Jones' "object of desire", Loe Kann, was also in analysis with Freud, who could barely conceal his erotic yearning for her. Meanwhile, Jones was in a relationship with Loe's nurse, Lina. Loe, soon after splitting up with Ernest, married "Jones II", his namesake Herbert. Their wedding was held in May 1914 in Budapest, with Freud attending.

Although Jones felt that he found "a much greater inner harmony" in his analysis (Jones, 1959, p. 189), Ferenczi thought that he needed further treatment; Freud agreed, but it did not happen. In the brief of his analysis, Jones had had to confront the humiliation of his short stature. Ferenczi told Bálint that

> he concentrated in the last sessions with Jones on his mother's insistence that he should be placed on quack milk substitutes which led to rickets and other serious side effects. In order to cope with the rejecting breast, his small stature, and lower class origins Ferenczi claimed that Jones had at the beginning of his career developed an omnipotence complex. At the time of his analysis he was slowly adjusting to that complex, becoming less forceful and more tactful. (Brome, 1983, p. 86)

Perhaps, in these sessions, there is a clue to why, as Roazen put it, Jones never quite forgave Ferenczi for being his analyst (Roazen, 1975, p. 359).

Jones was in analysis with Ferenczi during the summer of 1913, while Ferenczi was analysed by Freud for the first time in 1914. At the same time, this period was also a decisive one in the history of the psychoanalytical movement. Private lives began to get ever more entangled in complicated threads with the politics of the movement, and the schism with the great "dissidents", Adler, Stekel, and Jung, was all but complete. It is in this period that we find the plans to develop around Freud a sort of "praetorian guard", the so-called "Secret Committee" (in the summer of 1912), and its coming into being (November 1913).[2] The committee, whose original goal was the exclusion and isolation of Stekel and Jung, was born in the first instance of Ferenczi's and Jones' instigation, and the stages of this process are clearly visible in their correspondence. For example, "We must not give the Zurich lot time to take cover behind Freud's name and thus gain strength. The world should know of Jung's break [with Freud]. After all, one will find true 'psychoanalysis' where Freud is himself" (7F, p. 33).

Further developments

One of the signs of his friendship with Jones, developed during their analysis, is Ferenczi's complaint in his letter of 25th September 1913, that a "meaningless, confused and malicious" article, by a certain Albert Ehrenstein, appeared in *Pester Lloyd*, Budapest's leading German-language newspaper, reviewing an international congress of psychotherapy in Vienna, where Adler also spoke. Ferenczi asks Jones to write a few lines to

> your friend, J[ózsef] Vészi, the editor in chief of the P[ester] L[loyd], and ask him not to print every piece of nonsense about psychoanalysis that he receives. It would be better, though, if you were not to tell him that this idea comes from me; but you can let him know that in such questions, they can seek out my professional opinion. (4F, p. 17)

He goes on to add that he would try to get his friend, the well-known writer and literary critic, the editor of the review *Nyugat* and the co-founder of the Hungarian Psychoanalytical Society, Ignotus, to pen a reply to this "piece of trash". He refers to the deep impression that Jones made on Ignotus in Budapest, who "talks about you frequently and would like to see you again soon" (4F, p. 18). We do not know if Jones did, in fact, write the letter to József Vészi that Ferenczi asked him to.[3]

In search of a better understanding of transference phenomena, several contemporary analysts including Ferenczi turned towards telepathy with great curiosity and attention. In his letter of the 25th October 1913 (5F, pp. 25–26) Ferenczi brings to Jones' attention a couple (the mediums named as "Professor Alexander Roth and his wife") with whom Ferenczi was undertaking experiments in telepathy at the time.[4] The couple were to travel to Vienna, and then London; he asks Jones to arrange for the couple to be able to demonstrate their talents before the eminent London-based Society for Psychical Research. Here, we encounter a major difference between the two men. Ferenczi was fascinated and open-minded about seemingly paranormal phenomena: Rickman tells us that "he had been collecting data for years" (Rickman, 1933, p. 124). Jones was deeply sceptical. Ferenczi was a member of the Society for Psychical Research until his death, but Jones kept well away from it, despite the fact that many of his colleagues were associated with it.

Meanwhile, Ferenczi's efforts at academic acceptance suffered a severe blow. In his letter of the 16th December 1913, Ferenczi complains to Jones that his attempt to get a university readership (*Habilitation*) had failed: "[Professor Ernő] Jendrassik pulled out all the stops to ensure my downfall and he succeeded" (8F, p. 37).[5]

In 1914, until the outbreak of the First World War, Ferenczi wrote to Jones with some frequency. In his letter of the 16th March 1914, this is how he characterises life in Budapest: "Budapest is as always: full of enthusiasm for anything interesting, but without the stamina for hard work. I am beginning to think that I myself am of the Typus Budapestiensis" (9F, p. 42).

He complains to Jones that he misses their daily chats from the summer before, and that since Jones' departure from Budapest, he has not found another friend like him. He characterises his colleagues in the Association thus:

> Ignotus is busy with a thousand other things, little Radó is an intelligent chap, but very young still and essentially of a just critical disposition. It is true that in Dr. Hollós (consultant to the lunatic asylum in Nagyszeben) I have found a talented psychoanalyst, although he lives much too far away from here and his ambition complex irritates me now and then—perhaps because it collides with my own! (9F, p. 42)

The typed, officially stamped letter of the 20th May 1914[6] informs Jones that the previous day's general meeting of the Hungarian Psychoanalytical Association, with Sándor Radó as secretary and Ferenczi as president, elected him an honorary member.

> The President recalls warmly the pleasant relations, which developed during the summer of 1913 between the members of the Association and the current president of the London Group, Prof. Dr. Ernest Jones, who was in Budapest for an extended stay. In view of the great service Prof. Jones has done psychoanalysis, the President proposes to elect Prof. Dr. Ernest Jones an Honorary Member of the Association. The Annual General Meeting unanimously accepts the President's motion. (12F, p. 51)

The war years

Two months later, on the 20th July, Ferenczi informs Jones that he has definitely decided: he would visit England that summer (probably in the first week of August). He intends to spend most of his time in London, taking advantage of Jones' hospitality. "In return", he offers to continue Jones' analysis that they had begun in Budapest, during his stay, in the form of "completely standard analytic sessions" (14F, p. 59). Whether, and how, to continue Jones' analysis with Ferenczi becomes a recurring subject for years to come. These letters are of special value for historical research into the development of psychoanalytic methodology and theory. Through their negotiations of this issue, the picture of Ferenczi as analyst and Jones as his analysand comes alive, as we shall see in the later years of their correspondence.

On the 29th July 1914, Ferenczi is forced to inform Jones that he must renounce the "nice time" he hoped to have in London. Instead of his London plans, he is expecting his call-up papers: "It is quite possible I will have to report for military duty and join in the campaign as a physician, on horseback with the Hussars!!" (16F, p. 67). These papers duly arrived: Ferenczi joined the 7th Royal Pápa Hussar Regiment as its chief medical officer on the 24th October 1914.[7] Their correspondence did not, however, stop because of the war, even if they were citizens of two countries on opposite sides. Since the onset of war meant the end of direct postal communication between Britain and the Austro-Hungarian Empire, the correspondence continued via the Dutch psychoanalyst Jan van Emden. Freud and Jones used this same channel for their correspondence, and regularly exchanged letters throughout the four years of the Great War. His experiences of the war years as a military doctor put Ferenczi into the front line of psychoanalysts who attempted to understand and interpret the causes and dynamics of war neuroses and find possible ways for their treatment.

Two letters from Ferenczi to Jones are extant from this period. The first was written in Pápa on the 15th May 1915. In this letter, he thanks Jones for having finished the "arduous and boring" task of translating his writings, and then gives an account of his days in the military.

> I have nothing special to report about myself. Since the end of Oct[ober], I have been doing military service in a Hussar regiment, although only behind the lines for now, where there is little to do. I even see 2–3 private patients for analysis every day. Apart from that, I am thinking about problems on the frontier of psychology and biology; whether something useful will come of it is very much in doubt. Physically, I am very well, helped by the provincial calm and my daily rides. (17F, p. 69)

These "frontier problems" reflect his interest in Lamarck's phylogenetic theory and provide a theoretical framework for his famous *Thalassa: A Theory of Genitality* (Ferenczi, 1924[268]).

He further mentions that a professor from Salerno, (Marco) Levy (actually Levi)-Bianchini, is going to translate into Italian his paper on introjection. His observation on such a "strange contrast between this internationalisation and the current battles among nations!" are curiously current even today. The second extant Ferenczi letter from the war years is from the 24th July 1916. Ferenczi was by then serving in Budapest, at the Mária Valéria barracks hospital. In this letter, he foresees the end of the war and a reunion with Jones: "I believe that we will meet up again sooner than you think. I hear your first destination is Vienna. I want to be in the party!" (18F, p. 73).

None the less, behind the seemingly friendly tone of the letters, there lay suspicion and insecurity. Ferenczi, as we can see from his letters to Freud, sought systematically to undermine Jones with him. During the period of the breach with Jung, on the 6th August 1912, he warned Freud,

> The other Swiss are all too much under the influence of his [Jung's] suggestion, and they are all a bunch of anti-Semites.
>
> It has never been so clear to me as now what a psychic advantage there is in having been born a Jew and having remained protected in childhood from this atavistic nonsense. Even Putnam can easily relapse; you must always keep an eye on Jones and cut off his line of retreat. (*Freud–Ferenczi, 1*, p. 400)

As we can see from this letter, the Freud–Jung controversy mobilises anxiety and fear even among the most assimilated Jews in the psychoanalytical community; the shadow of anti-Semitism is cast upon not only professional relations, but personal ones as well.

Mistrust was aggravated by an ensuing conflict between Ferenczi and Jones over originality and authorship. On the 26th December 1915, he wrote the following to Freud:

> Jones's tendency to plagiarize is familiar to me; he once appropriated my essay on suggestion in a similar way. His originality is (as I know from the analysis) inhibited; for that reason he has to satisfy his ambition in this way. Despite all that, he is a good boy—only one has to correct him in this respect. (*Freud–Ferenczi, 2*, p. 99)

The accusation of plagiarism against Jones goes back to his 1910 paper, "The action of suggestion in psychotherapy" (Jones, 1910a, 1911). At the time, however, the question of plagiarism was not yet raised; in fact, as we saw earlier, Ferenczi even thanked Jones, in his letter of the 8th April 1911, for being so complimentary about his work on suggestion. The accusation of plagiarism none the less played an important role in their conflicts in the 1920s and the cooling of their relationship.[8]

Growing mistrust

The much-anticipated reunion between Jones and Ferenczi finally took place on 24th September 1919 in Vienna. However, the great joy of seeing each other again after the war years was soon overshadowed by the conflicts and disagreements of the 1920s, which the history of psychoanalysis knows as the "Rank debates". Otto Rank's book *Das Trauma der Geburt und seine Bedeutung für die Psychanalyse* (*The Trauma of Birth and Its Significance for Psychoanalysis*) (1924) had a central role in this, as well as the publication and reception of Ferenczi and Rank's joint work, *Entwicklungsziele der Psychanalyse: zur Wechselbeziehung zwischen Theorie und Praxis* (Developmental Aims of Psychoanalysis: On the Inter-relation between Theory and Practice) (*The Development of Psychoanalysis*, 1925). The controversy, combined with other passionate debates, polarised the members of the "Secret Committee", entangled the lines, and created personal conflicts alongside the professional ones.[9] Finally, all these led to the dissolution of the "Secret Committee". We can follow this process in the circular correspondence of the "Secret Committee".

Jones' and Ferenczi's relationship was complicated not only by the roles they played in the "committee", and changes in those roles, but also by personal tensions and passions which previously only found expression indirectly. The accusation of plagiarism resurfaced, and Freud, for his part, more than once called Ferenczi's attention to Jones' "real defects in character and behaviour with which one can't confront him quite honestly and which he must conceal by means of some arrangement or other" (*Freud–Ferenczi, 3*, p. 90). As for the "audacious and clumsy" English, he notes that "Collaboration with them is not very possible. When they are alone, they will probably do it well, in any case better. Jones is in many respects a personality unsuited to be a leader" (*Freud–Ferenczi, 3*, p. 93). Clearly, it was on the basis of this and similar impressions that Freud came to the conclusion that we find in his circular letter of 26th November 1922: "Jones should finish that short course of analysis that he once began with Ferenczi" (*Die Rundbriefe, 3*, p. 232, in Wittenberger & Tögel, 2003).

The dramatic clash of personal issues took place at the August 1923 meeting of the "Secret Committee", held in Freud's absence, in San Cristoforo, Italy. The meeting was stamped by Rank's and Jones' extraordinarily sharp disagreement. Rank was angry about an anti-Semitic remark Jones made about him to Brill, and demanded that Jones be excluded from the committee, which did not come to pass thanks to Abraham's intervention. Jones reported this episode to his wife Katherine thus:

> We have spent the whole day thrashing out the Rank–Jones affair. Very painful but I hope our relations will now be better and believe so, but on the other hand expect Ferenczi will hardly speak to me for Brill has just been there and told him I had said Rank was a swindling Jew (stark übertrieben [grossly exaggerated]). Brill of course has gone back to U.S.A. without seeing me. (quoted in Brome, 1983, p. 139)

He added,

> The whole community, after hours of talking and shouting . . . decided that I was in the wrong in the Rank–Jones affair, in fact that I am neurotic. A Jewish family council sitting on one sinner must be a great affair, but picture it when the whole five are insisting on analysing him on the spot and altogether! (quoted in Brome, 1983, p. 139)

No wonder that remarks of an anti-Semitic flavour created such havoc. Bearing in mind that since the Middle Ages anti-Semitism has been an ever-present undercurrent in Europe, seemingly paranoid reactions can be seen in a different light. By the 1920s, Central Europe had experienced a revival of anti-Semitic attitudes, movements, and political measures. In Germany, Nazism was on the rise, and, in fact, Hungary was the first country in Europe after the war to introduce anti-Jewish laws: the *numerus clausus* law, limiting the number of Jewish students to be admitted to universities, came into effect as early as 1920 (see, for example, Kovács, 1994).

Ferenczi wrote this to Jones after the events of San Cristoforo, on the 7th October 1923:

> . . . I can only repeat what I have already said several times in San Cristoforo: I do not consider you an out-and-out neurotic either, but am firmly of the opinion that you are in need of analysis, not only

> because of your, as I believe, unconsciously motivated actions, but also because I must consider your previous analysis incomplete just on the grounds of my technique having been far less perfected at the time. I thus think further analysis desirable, if for no other reason than for the sake of your own analytic practice. However, if we were to start a proper analysis this time, we should not (although my analyses are much shorter these days) allow it to be constrained by any predetermination of length or termination date. How this might fit with the demands of your life I am, of course, unable to judge. (24F, p. 92)

Jones took his time mulling over Ferenczi's offer and replied almost a year later, on the 7th August 1924.

> You will have guessed that the reason for the delay was that various matters, such as our unhappy suggestion controversy and the subsequent events connected with the Congress, made it inexpedient to enter into such personal matters, whereas now I feel freer to do so. I had and still have a strong desire to continue the analysis, chiefly because the most perfect attainable is the ideal we should all aim at in connection with psycho-analysis. On the other hand, the continuing expenses of my life and arrangements here make it absolutely impossible to be away from my work for more than the shortest time, which would obviously not be satisfactory. I can only console myself with the thought that anyone who is so happy in his love-life as I am and able to work so satisfactorily cannot be in any urgent need of further analysis, and I am sure you would agree with this criterion. (28J, p. 104)

When Jones wrote this letter, the shockwaves caused by Rank's and then Ferenczi's and Rank's common work were already at their most severe. In this letter, he reproaches Ferenczi with grave censures for his co-operation with Rank. "I really fear he is repeating the history of Jung, and for the same neurotic reasons. No-one identifies you with him in this respect, though it is a real puzzle to know how you came to write a book in common" (28J, p. 103).

Ferenczi answered Jones' accusation a few days later. In his letter of the 18th August, he states,

> You are absolutely right to say you must not identify me with Rank completely, when it comes to scientific matters; such complete identity is rare in science, especially where new ideas, like the ones Rank develops in his book on birth trauma, are concerned. My "Genital

> Theory" would acknowledge the moment of birth somewhat differently; it also does not discuss the vicissitudes of this moment in the neuroses. And it is exactly this point over which I do not (or not yet) agree wholly with Rank's position, even although I am convinced he has added a great deal to what we know. It will be the task of further examination and research to bring Rank's idea into harmony with the main body of ps[ycho]a[nalytic] knowledge. (29F, p. 107)

In this letter, Ferenczi also assures Jones that he understands the reasons for which he does not wish to continue the analysis they had begun eleven years earlier, and ends thus: "So far, we have been burning up and freezing by turns. But we enjoy the peace" (29F, p. 108).

Hot and cold

But there was not much peace to be had. Ferenczi and Jones continued their correspondence between 1924 and 1933; in these letters, too, they are alternately "hot and cold". Personal motives and, frequently, personal insults were often the end result of the great debates then dividing the psychoanalytical movement (such as the relations between the Central European branch of the movement—Vienna, Berlin, Budapest—and the English and American branches, as well as the question of dominance, "lay analysis", and the technical questions of psychoanalysis, etc.). Their conflicts, however, did not prevent Ferenczi from approaching Jones for favours: for example, for help with Géza Róheim's planned visit to England (see letter 31F, p. 115).

The report Ferenczi gives to Freud from Baden-Baden on the 30th June 1927 of his first visit to England is also a document of ambivalent feelings, which tainted the whole experience:

> We spent twelve days in London; almost the entire time was devoted to invitations, lectures, conversations with individuals. Jones strove to heap every conceivable personal honour (in contrast to the American reception) upon me. (Meeting of the British group, with the request to lecture something to them; several large dinners, even a garden party in Jones's nice house.) Naturally, my former pupils Inman, Eder, Cole, used the occasion to testify to their friendship. The actual conversation with Jones took place in his country house in Elstead. I was mindful of your warning 'Be careful.' Actually, I found Jones's statements lacking in full and complete honesty. (*Freud–Ferenczi*, *3*, p. 311)

Mutual mistrust prevails, but it does not stop Ferenczi acknowledging and thanking Jones for the "amazing welcome" he had received from Jones and his wife, which—as he writes a few days before, on the 26th June—was not only addressed to him, but also to "the Cause" (die Sache) (35F, p. 131).

On the 6th January 1930, Ferenczi turns to Jones in a hard, bitter letter (unfortunately we do not have Jones' letter to which this is the reply):

> The ambivalence of which you speak is undeniable, but the feeling is quite mutual. Your ambiguous behaviour with regards to the question of lay analysis (!) has contributed a great deal to the increase in negativity on my part. Even though you yourself are president of a group with lay members, you acted not (!) infrequently in a manner designed to encourage the opponents of lay [analysts], e.g. at the Innsbruck Congress. . . .
>
> I am left with no other option than to return the compliment, of my contribution being unconscious and therefore analysable (!), with all due respect. It may be that an effort on both sides could remove the undeniable obstacles from our path. But, seeing we are exchanging home truths, I must make a comment on your writings, too. I also do not read your work with undivided pleasure. If my papers are wild and fantastical, yours often give the impression of a kind of logical–sadistic violence, particularly since the, by the way, equally fantastical papers on child analysis appeared, I have not been enamoured with your English group at all. You see, there was enough tension in the air; perhaps this exchange of letters will mark the beginning of an improvement in our relationship. (39F, p. 146)[10]

In Ferenczi's entry in his *Clinical Diary* for the 2nd October 1932, he says, "I have just received a few personally friendly lines from Jones. He has sent roses, suggested a circular letter" (Ferenczi, 1988, p. 257). Exactly two months before his death, he wrote the following to Jones,

> As to your question about winter and spring, I have to tell you that I had a rather trying winter but am looking forward to spring hopefully. Your roses seem to have endured the winter rather nicely, at least I hope so because the winter season was rather mild. I hope the roses will often remind me of both you and your beautiful country-place. (22 March 1933, letter no. 43F, p. 163)

Barely a month after Ferenczi's death, on the 24th June 1933, Jones writes to Paul Federn about the need to write "our dear friend" Ferenczi's biography, evaluating and appreciating both his personality and the significance of his scientific work (BPAS Archives, PO4/C/C/01). This biography was never completed; none the less, Jones continued an extensive correspondence with Michael Bálint during the writing of his Freud biography (Jones & Balint, 2004). The "codified" portrait of Ferenczi which appears in Jones' biography of Freud is a story of half a century, since it sealed fifty years of Jones and Ferenczi's relationship. Now, fifty years later, far removed from the historical era in which Ferenczi and Jones lived, it seems worthwhile to re-evaluate their relationship, in order to show how the relationship of these two important figures of the early history of psychoanalysis, both to each other and to the movement, breaks through the cracks of a codified memory.

In his biography of Freud, Ernest Jones depicts Ferenczi in the last struggles of his life as "mentally ill" and "paranoid". This diagnosis, which Fromm thought of as "character assassination", contributed a great deal to the marginalisation of Ferenczi's methods and oeuvre in the psychoanalytical movement. But such stigmatising rumour was not Jones' invention alone. Some of the leading personalities of the psychoanalytical movement of the time reported similar opinions in their private discourse and letters. For example, Freud wrote to Jones on the 29th May 1933, shortly after Ferenczi's death,

> [F]or years Ferenczi has no longer been with us, indeed, not even with himself. It is now easier to comprehend the slow process of destruction to which he fell victim. During the last two years it expressed itself organically in pernicious anaemia, which soon led to severe motor disturbances. Liver therapy improved the condition of his blood, but had no effect on the other symptoms. In his last weeks he could no longer walk or stand at all. Simultaneously a mental degeneration in the form of paranoia developed with uncanny logical consistency. Central to this was the conviction that I did not love him enough, did not want to acknowledge his work, and also that I had analyzed him badly. His technical innovations were connected with this, as he wanted to show me how lovingly one has to treat one's patients in order to help them. (*Freud–Jones*, p. 721)

As if such treatment were not enough, shortly after Ferenczi's death Jones reneged on his agreement to publish Ferenczi's

"Confusion of tongues" paper in the *International Journal*, at the instigation of Joan Riviere. Jones did not take much persuading, but again he was not alone in being embarrassed by the paper. Freud had tried to prevent Ferenczi reading it at the Wiesbaden Congress in 1932. It is a sad end to the complex relationship charted in this correspondence.

Notes

1. On Jones's biography, see Brome, 1983; Maddox, 2006.
2. On the history of the "Secret Committee" see, for example, Grosskurth, 1991.
3. On this affair see Note 7 to 4F (25 September 1913) letter, p. 20.
4. See also Note 1 to 8F (16 December 1913) letter, p. 38.
5. On Jendrassik and Ferenczi's failure to get university title see Erős, 2011.
6. See this document in the present volume (p. 53).
7. On Ferenczi's military carrier see Erős, 2010.
8. On the accusations of plagiarism see Note 3 to 25F (13 January 1924) letter, p. 96.
9. See Bókay, 1998; Rudnytsky, Bókay, & Giampieri, 1996.
10. On the background of this letter see Notes 2 and 3 to letter no. 39F, p. 147.

Challenges of honesty

Gábor Szőnyi

There was one thing to which Sándor Ferenczi was committed more than to Freud: psychoanalysis. Above all others, he took the *method* extremely seriously, not in a descriptive sense, but by following its spirit and exploring it in its totality.

Freud proposed taking mental phenomena as facts that can be studied, and practised self-analysis. He experienced the pain of honesty towards oneself, and said that self-analysis has limits.

Nowadays, self-analysis is seen as one of the most important tools of an analyst; however, Freud did not place self-analysis among the central prerequisites in undertaking psychoanalysis, and, in the period before the IPA organised training, we do not find it as a requirement for future analysts. Training analysis was introduced, and then supervision. From that point on, honesty was taken for granted. The requirements demanded more and more analysis, because any failure or incompetence of an analyst—both in conducting therapy and participating in analytic organisations—were seen as failings of their personal analysis.

Ferenczi could never obtain the quantity of analysis for himself that he was longing for, and he was the advocate of "super-analysis", which aimed to remove all the "blind spots" of future analysts.

Ferenczi was willing to explore the whole domain of the basic rule: express—without any filtering—what you have on your mind. His personality was that of a researcher, for whom experimentation is natural.

The famous—and scarily misunderstood—experiences with mutual analysis explored the limits of honesty in free association for both actors, the analysand and the analyst. Ferenczi said that honesty in free associating has limits, and, although both actors struggle with internal and external honesty, the roles in the setting are not interchangeable.

There are, today, three settings where the honesty of an analyst is at stake: his/her personal analysis, supervisions/case discussions, and the analyses he/she conducts. These require the capacity and *the willingness* to be honest.

Being honest can always turn into a painful exercise. It is not just a given, even if the capacity is broad and the analyst has extensive training. *Willingness* to be honest needs to be rebuilt in every context again and again—which is a crucial point of self-analysis. Being in personal analysis, the candidate's struggle with honesty is part of the process of interaction between defences and conflicting urges. His/her associative self-exploration is also a kind of self-analysis, in the presence of, and shared with, the personal analyst. In an analysis which one conducts, the struggle fought for maintenance of self-analysis in the presence of, but not shared with, another person—the patient—depends highly on a willingness to be honest that can be assessed only from inside. Analytic supervision is a special place, *where self-analysis*—in connection with the patient and the analytic process—*can be practised* in the presence of, and shared with, another person—the supervisor. This depends heavily on how much space for associative analytic working attitude phases is included in the supervision session.

Ferenczi criticised the hypocrisy of doctors, and honesty, indispensable in self-analysis, is the opposite of hypocrisy. It is worth reviewing our training practices to see how much they help or hinder the growing capacity to be honest and the willingness to practise honesty in our daily work. A hundred years of the work of the British and Hungarian Societies bear witness to the struggles to disclose or hide truth in practical work and in organisational life.

Around this correspondence

André Haynal

Si duo faciunt idem non est idem (if two (people) do the same, it is not the same) says the Latin proverb. The letters in this book show a beautiful example of two men, both interested in one's inner life, exploring ways to help other human beings and also, possibly, themselves. With this purpose, they both strive to be part of Freud's inner circle: two men so similar, but, nevertheless, so different.

Sándor Ferenczi's family originated from territories belonging to Austria (now Poland) in the Austro-Hungarian Empire (Habsburg Empire). He considered himself Hungarian, although he spoke Yiddish, a German dialect, with his mother, and studied medicine at the Vienna University.

He was part of the light-hearted Budpest *bohème*, for whom inner freedom was one of the highest ideals and fantasy an important value. His professional life took place close to literary and artistic circles. Developing rich mutual relationships through what he called *introjection*, he considered cementing solidarity as the best possible achievement of human development. Central to this was what he called "sincerity" with others and himself—what would later be called authenticity. It was a way of life where the inner person should match the outer conduct. He conceptually opposed this to "hypocrisy", meaning, to him, hiding one's true personality.

Many have written about his long and close relationship with Freud; indeed, he might have been the closest of Freud's followers. They had many emotional ties, even though, in the 1920s and the beginning of the 1930s until the end of Ferenczi's life (1933), they were deeply involved in heated and sometimes painful controversial scientific discussions.

On the other side of the correspondence, Ernest Jones, Welsh, serious, and professional, lived in a more real world. His concerns were in outside realities, whether this was the dimension of scientific truth or of organisational problems and solutions (in the medical establishment). Born in Wales, in an environment of *petite-bourgeoisie*, he was the son of a colliery engineer. Educated at Cardiff University and at the University College London (UCL), he received a first-class honours degree in medicine, followed by a public health diploma from Cambridge (1905).

Eventually, he became a leading psychoanalyst, the president of the British Society, and, subsequently, the president of the world-wide professional organisation (IPA).

Jones contributed important theoretical considerations to psychoanalytic literature, where Ferenczi suggested more nuanced details. Ferenczi's concerns reflected his practice and his striving to ameliorate psychoanalytic activity, while Jones' reflected his institutional and academic preoccupations. Ferenczi reminds us more of the Shakespearian "There are more things in heaven and earth . . ." (Hamlet, Act 1, Scene V) so often quoted in Central Europe.

Jones' ideal was a decent human being with a calm scientific background. The reality-orientated Welshman contributed essentially to the spreading of psychoanalysis in the world, especially in the English-speaking countries. In a labour of love and of detailed knowledge, his Freud biography collects and presents amazing details of Freud's thinking and of his life.

He was the resolute leader of the British Society, even in the years of great internal tensions. His style was quite different from the looser, less organised formal training in Budapest, although Ferenczi's informal manners in fields such as psychoanalytical education and interpersonal relationships in general had a stimulating influence but also provoked criticism.

With the exception of some episodes where the tensions come to the fore, their correspondence reflects these differences in character and opinion without becoming explicit about them. The correspondence begins like a Shakespearian drama, but without ever reaching a really dramatic point. For example, in the San Cristoforo incident, Jones allegedly called Rank a "swindling Jew" (see Foreword in this volume), while Ferenczi kept a middle position in the group.

The similarities and differences of these two personalities prefigure the wide range of the people attracted to psychoanalysis and who contribute in different ways to its development with a shared deep conviction in human perfectibility. This also unites the descendants of the pioneers of the British and the Hungarian Societies.

LETTERS

1F

DR. FERENCZI SÁNDOR BUDAPEST, VII, ERZSÉBET-KÖRÚT 54.

Budapest, 8 April 1911

Dear Friend[1]

I too must content myself with the English salutation and have to write the letter itself in a language I am more familiar with. My thanks for having remembered me, for sending proof of your diligent and productive psychoanalytic activity, and for your detailed and appreciative review of my work on suggestion.[2] With professor Freud, we often talked about our friends in America and took pleasure from this small but steadfast group of supporters across the ocean.

Psychoanalysis—once unleashed—is like energy, it cannot be destroyed. It will not leave people in peace until they come to terms with it. It is no use to struggle or resist; its biggest enemies are those who suffer most from its revelations; Ziehen,[3] Kräpelin[4] and Oppenheim[5] must have to dream psychoanalysis, given their rejection of it by day.

I myself am well. Unfortunately, I have too many analytic hours and therefore write too little—my all too abundant experience has hardly been put to use on paper this year. It makes me admire your capacity for work all the more.

Next Thursday, I will travel to Tyrol with Professor Freud. He is looking for a summer house there for his family. I very much look forward to our spending this time together.[6]

In Vienna, Adler[7] (seconded by Stekel[8]) is beginning to take up a particular scientific position: he overemphasises the organic, the self-preservative drive—and scotomises sexuality in a rather tendentious fashion.

One must fear that those who do not altogether have a firm grasp of things themselves, might keep them company in this "reactionary" departure.

I hope your letter betokens the beginning of a regular correspondence and that you will come over for the congress (due to be held in Weimar[9]).

Kindest regards,

Ferenczi

Wilhelm Stekel (1868–1940).

Notes to letter 1F

1. In English in the original.
2. "Introjektion und Übertragung. Eine psychoanalytische Studie: 1. Die Introjektion in der Neurose. 2. Die Rolle der Übertragung bei der Hypnose und bei der Suggestion" (Ferenczi, 1909[67]) appeared in the *Jahrbuch* (*1*[1909]: 422–457), and was translated by Jones in *Contributions to Psycho-Analysis* with the title: "Introjection and transference. 1. Introjection in the neuroses. 2. The part played by transference in hypnotism and suggestion" (Ferenczi, 1916[186], pp. 35–93). Ferenczi might be thanking Jones for sending him his "The action of suggestion in psychotherapy" (Jones, 1911), which had been published in January in the *Journal of Abnormal Psychology*. If so, he would change his mind about Jones' paper, coming to see it as plagiarising his own work (see Ferenczi's letter to Freud, 26 December, 1915 in *Freud–Ferenczi, 2*, p. 99, on the accusation of plagiarism see also 25F, note 3).
3. Theodor Ziehen (1862–1950), was a German psychiatrist and experimental psychologist with a special interest in child psychology. For an account of his antipathy towards psychoanalysis, see, for example, the letter from Karl Abraham to Sigmund Freud, 10 November 1908 in *Freud–Abraham*, p. 64.
4. Emil Kraepelin (1856–1926), a German psychiatrist, was Professor of Psychiatry at Munich University from 1903 to 1922. The system of classification for psychiatric disorders he devised was enormously influential, most notably his subdivision of the psychoses into dementia praecox (schizophrenia) on the one hand, and manic–depressive insanity on the other. His principal work, *Psychiatrie. Ein Lehrbuch für Studierende und Ärtze* (Psychiatry. A Text book for Students and Physicians), remained authoritative for a long time and went through many editions. For a brief sketch of his opposition to psychoanalysis at this time, see Falzeder and Burnham (2007, pp. 1226, 1234).
5. Hermann Oppenheim (1858–1919), a German neurologist, was head of the "Berliner Privatpolyklinik für Nervenkranke", a private clinic for the mentally ill, which became a centre for training and further education for physicians from all over the world. In 1907, he founded the Society for German Neurologists with Wilhelm Erb. For a brief sketch of his opposition to psychoanalysis at this time, see Falzeder and Burnham (2007, p. 1227).
6. Ferenczi and Freud spent two days (16th and 17th April) in Bozen, Southern Tyrol (now Bolzano, Italy). (See Freud's letter to Jung dated 11 April 1911 in *Freud–Jung*, p. 415. See also Freud's letter on 10 April and

Ferenczi's letter on 11 and 24 April 1911, in *Freud–Ferenczi, 1*, pp. 268–270).

7. Alfred Adler (1870–1937), a physician, was a member of the circle around Freud from 1902 and the first significant follower of Freud to break away, in 1911, and found his own school of "Individual Psychology". After 1926, he frequently worked in the USA, moving there permanently in 1935. He died in Aberdeen, during a lecture tour in May 1937. According to Jones, Freud had stepped down as leader of the Viennese to make Adler the President of the Vienna Psychoanalytic Association and had given Adler and Stekel control over the *Zentralblatt*, newly founded in the autumn of 1910. Freud had done so in an attempt to appease the Viennese, who were disgruntled both by his preference for Jung and by Ferenczi's speech at the Nuremberg Congress proposing Jung as first President of the International Psychoanalytical Association (see *Jones, 2*, pp. 75–76).
8. Wilhelm Stekel (1868–1940), a neurologist, was one of the first members of the "Wednesday Society", following his analysis with Freud. He became known in the psychoanalytic movement chiefly for his work on the interpretation of dreams and symbols. Freud made him Adler's deputy as Vice-President of the Vienna Society in the wake of the Nuremberg Congress. He split from Freud and his circle in 1912 but remained editor (at first jointly with Alfred Adler) of the *Zentralblatt* until 1914. In 1923, he founded the "Organisation of Independent Medical Analysts", came out against lay analysis, and developed "Active Analysis". He spent his last years in London, where he committed suicide. On Stekel's life and his conflict with Freud, see Bos and Groenendijk, 2007; Gutheil, 1950; Nitzschke, 1992.
9. The third International Congress of Psychoanalysis took place in Weimar on 21 and 22 September 1911. Jones attended it. Originally, Jung wanted to hold it first in Lugano, then in Nürnberg.

2F

DR. FERENCZI SÁNDOR BUDAPEST, VII, ERZSÉBET-KÖRÚT 54.

Budapest, 14 November 1911

Dear Friend,

We are each required to take account of our level of linguistic proficiency,—everything stays as it is: you will write to me in English and I shall write to you in German.—You surprised me again with a whole host of concepts, for which I thank you very much; they caused me to be amazed at the stamina with which you do not cease to produce such quantities[1] of work, and work of such qualitative value.

The other things you wrote about are pleasing too. Freud is likely to be right with his assumption that a personal complex has played a role for me. In any case, you must make this attempt—and do not hesitate for too long. I hope your success will justify Freud.

My lymphangoitis made the journey home rather arduous, since I did not manage to secure a sleeper. Though four days of bed rest put everything right again.

—Now to your questions,[2] which I shall hardly be able to answer satisfactorily.

1.) It is without doubt that large doses of alcohol anaesthetise all mental activity and thus the libido as well; all of the limbs of the very drunk are paralysed, they are probably "impotent in actual fact". Smaller doses only cause the anaesthesia of psychic inhibitions: one is "animated" and "spirited". Slightly larger quantities paralyse ethical censorship and destroy sublimation. (Homosexuality and all other perversions appear in un-sublimated form; homosexuality is so conspicuous because too much of it is sublimated.) Chronic alcoholism brings with it chronic[3] damage to the sublimations, which outlasts individual episodes of intoxication. "Alcoholic impotence" may also be promoted by an emergence of discrete perversions (homosexuality, oral and anal eroticism, sadism, etc), which disturbs the synthesis of sexual components and deprives the genital zone of its dominance. I may have to write about these things, since Bleuler[4] is planning to attack me from a point of view on abstinence.[5]

2.) Jealousy is always the "categorical imperative of exclusivity". This has been known forever. I had not realised that |: in line with the 'two-some' of parents :| one loves to be loved by at least two[6] simultaneously; indeed, one wishes to get rid of the obstacle between the two who want to love each other, and maintain the love of both.

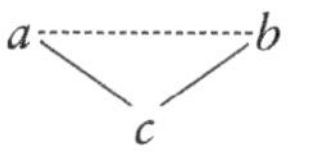

That is, one likes to live in a triangular relationship, at the point of the triangle (c), from where one can love a and b while simultaneously keeping them apart. The infantile situation with regards to father and mother is like that of a jealous affair with a married woman, where the cuckolded husband is empathised with at the same time. Since the latter component (homosexuality) is usually repressed, by ways of compensation the love for the woman has to be exaggerated, while homosexuality is projected as jealousy.

Even the husband (b) is quite happy with this, since from his position he too can, unconsciously and regressively, re-live the infantile situation.

Women know well that dying love may be rekindled by flirting with another man such that it provokes jealousy. The explanation[7] that the woman regains her value for us when we see others in love with her is a rationalisation. Only the Oedipus constellation actually explains the matter.

Husbands are "blind" when it comes to the wife's 'gentleman friend'. Why? Because they are happy in this threesome and do not wish to change the situation.

3.) As to "persecution mania"; I do not know more than what is written in the Jahrbuch about this.

4.) Ambisexual phase or period might be serviceable for ambisexuality.

5.) Of course a fear of sweating does not always mean homosexuality.—I have found it in all homosexuals.

6.) Admiration for women can be the result of drive-repression,[8] and thus genuine, but it may also be a kind of false, screaming erotomania—that is a cover for homosexuality. The cultural climate prevailing in the United States has the effect of 1.) repressing heterosexuality (hence: admiration for women), 2.) favouring (usually well-sublimated) homosexuality (sports, intimate friendships, politics, work teams). To guard against the encroachment of homosexuality, women are then worshipped and admired in an even more exaggerated fashion.

That is all I can say in response to your questions. You see, things are[9] still incomplete.

Cordially,
Ferenczi

P.S. Jealousy may have the following possibilities:

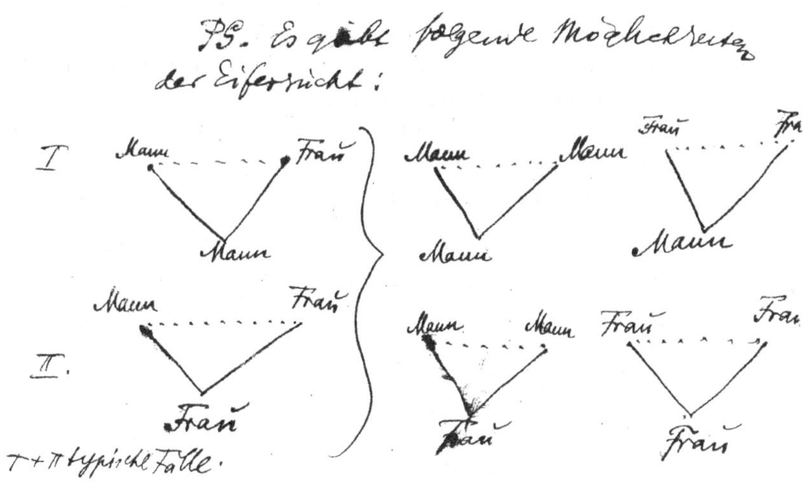

I + II typical cases [Mann=man; Frau=woman]

Notes to letter 2F

1. Corrected in the original from "such quality".
2. The questions probably occurred to Jones while reading Ferenczi's paper "Über die Rolle der Homosexualität in der Pathogenese der Paranoia" which was published in the *Jahrbuch* (*3*: 101–119), and was translated by Jones with title: "On the part played by homosexuality in the pathogenesis of paranoia" (Ferenczi, 1911[80]).
3. Corrected in the original from "permanent".
4. Eugen Bleuler (1857–1939) was Professor of Psychiatry at Zurich university from 1898 to 1926 and Director of the psychiatric clinic, the "Burghölzli". With Freud, he published the *Jahrbuch für psychoanalytische und psychopathologische Forschungen*. His *Lehrbuch der Psychiatrie* (*Textbook of Psychiatry*) remains authoritative to this day (Bleuler, 1916).
5. Bleuler, like his predecessor at the Burghölzi, August Forel, was a leading figure in the anti-alcohol movement. In a footnote to his paper "Über die Rolle der Homosexualität in der Pathogenese der Paranoia" ("On the part played by homosexuality in the pathogenesis of paranoia") (Ferenczi, 1911[80]), Ferenczi had argued that "The one-sided agitation of temperance reformers tries to veil the fact that in the large majority of cases alcoholism is not the cause of neuroses, but a result of them, and a calamitous one" (Ferenczi, 1916[186], p. 163). Bleuler's polemic in reply to Ferenczi's paper was published as "Alkohol und Neurosen (Alcohol and neurosis)" in *Jahrbuch, 3*: 848–852 (Bleuler, 1911), followed by Ferenczi's response "Alkohol und Neurosen. Antwort auf eine Kritik des Herrn Professor E. Bleuler" (Alcohol and neurosis. A reply to the criticisms of Prof. Eugen Bleuler) (*Jahrbuch, 3*: 853–857) (Ferenczi, 1911[81]).
6. Corrected in the original from "several".
7. Corrected in the original from "idea".
8. In the original, "drive" was inserted later.
9. Difficult to decipher in the original.

3F

DR. FERENCZI SÁNDOR BUDAPEST, VII, ERZSÉBET-KÖRÚT 54.

i.e. 2 November 1912[1]

Dear Colleague,

I thank you for the attentiveness of sending me your paper on anxiety.[2] I consider this to be the first act on your part to result from our Committee meeting.[3] I shall comment as honestly as I can and ask you to do likewise in relation to myself, should the situation arise.

The paper is very beautiful and rich in thought. Since Stekel has denied[4] the existence of the actual neuroses,[5] the problem may be termed "topical", even if in the current circumstances, it would be more in keeping with the times to foreground the pure cases, the prototypes. After all, the existence of predominantly psychogenic and predominantly toxic symptom-complexes is not in doubt, and they lend themselves to an examination of what is specifically psychogenic and what is specifically toxic, though there are, of course, no "pure cultures" in reality. (You could emphasise this in your paper.)

I should like to share with you some ideas, surely all of them familiar to yourself, the inclusion of which I would, however, consider advisable (especially for didactic purposes).

1.) You might emphasise that the question as to the existence of pure "psychogeneity" is more of a philosophical one. In fact, the psyche may only be looked at psychologically and the body only from the point of view of the natural sciences etc. (Although I consider this comment to be neither important nor absolutely necessary.)

2.) Psychoneurosis does not necessarily have to turn into anxiety neurosis (despite abstinence), since its symptoms also represent a hidden kind of sexual gratification.[6] (Freud) (Hysteria + bisexuality, *kl. Schriften*)[7]

3.) The words "whipped up" are part of Adler's sadistic terminology; they should be cut.[8]

4.) You should emphasise that your anxiety instinct is not a departure from Freud's assumption that the transformation of anxiety (transformation of libido into anxiety) is carried out by the ego, in this case mastering an internal danger in the same way it usually masters external ones. (Your nightmare produced plenty of evidence for this!)[9]

In any case, it is very good that you tackle this problem and do not leave it to the enemy. For Stekel is, as of late, openly opposed. He resigned from the Association, Prof. Freud has withdrawn as publisher of the Zentralblatt, is founding a new Zentralblatt and wants to make me its editor. I have accepted the proposal. It is still uncertain whether a Berlin publishing house, Deuticke,[10] or Heller[11] will become its publishers.[12] All this is to be kept secret. The Viennese are happy about Stekel's resignation—Prof. Freud is delighted with it.—

I am reading Jung's paper, which was given to me to review.[13] Sadly, I am not altogether fit for work: a small abscess has infected many of my lymphatic glands and I have had a fever for the last two weeks or so.

I am sending you the paper, in case you should like to decide in favour of the suggested additions. You could write them in English; I would add the German translation where you wish.—The paper would be for the new journal, which is why I have kept it.

Warmest regards,
Ferenczi

I hope, we will be published in January!

Notes to letter 3F

1. The date "i.e. 2/11/12" is in an unknown hand. The letter was probably written around 6 November 1912 (see *Freud–Ferenczi, 1,* pp. 425, 426 note 1, 427).
2. Jones had read "Die Beziehung zwischen Angstneurose und Angsthysterie" ("The relation between anxiety neurosis and anxiety hysteria") at the International Society for Medical Psychology and Psychotherapy in Zurich on 9 September. It was published in the *Zeitschrift* and *Journal of Abnormal Psychology* (Jones, 1913).
3. The "Secret Committee" did not meet officially until 25 May 1913. This must refer to an earlier informal meeting. The members of the Committee agreed "that if anyone wished to depart from any of the fundamental tenets of psychoanalytical theory (. . .) he would promise not to do so publicly before first discussing his views with the rest" (*Jones,* 2, p. 172). Jones had sent his paper through its translator Seif by 3 November 1912 when Ferenczi commented on it in a letter to Freud and mentioned that Jones had sent a card pressing him for a critique (see *Freud–Ferenczi, 1,* p. 425). Ferenczi notes that Jones sent it "evidently in honest observance of the Vienna accords" so that Ferenczi could indicate points of departure from Freud. Jones had presented his paper at The Third Annual Meeting of the International Society for Medical Psychology and Psychotherapy in Zurich on 9 September, 1912, and had already submitted it to Stekel for publication in the *Zentralblatt.* Following Stekel's secession from Freud, he withdrew it so that it could be published in the new *Zeitschrift* edited by Ferenczi and Rank which appeared in early 1913.
4. Corrected in the original from "claimed".
5. Freud had supplied an introduction to the first edition of *Nervöse Angstzustände und ihre Behandlung* (*Conditions of Nervous Anxiety and their Treatment*) (Stekel, 1908; Freud, 1908f). In the second edition (1912) Stekel departed from Freud's views, dispensing with the actual neuroses. Freud (1912f) marked out his disagreement with Stekel with respect to the actual neuroses in "Contributions to a discussion on masturbation" (see *S.E., 12*: p. 248). For Stekel's own view of these events, see his "On the history of the analytical movement" (originally "Zur Geschichte der analytischen Bewegung") (Stekel, 1926).
6. In his letter to Freud about Jones's paper on 3 November 1912 Ferenczi had commented: "Some points are simply erroneous, as is the idea that *hysteria,* because it has abstinence (impotence) as a consequence, must produce *anxiety neurosis* along the way. Jones forgets that psychoneurosis is not only a hindrance to normal sexual satisfaction but is itself a form

of sexual satisfaction, so only that part of the repressed libido that cannot gain expression in psychoneurotic symptoms must be transformed into anxiety" (*Freud–Ferenczi, 1*, p. 425). As Ferenczi notes later in his letter he kept Jones's paper with a view to including it in the new *Zeitschrift*. Jones took on board Ferenczi's suggested alterations. Here he qualified his argument that infantile conflicts underlying hysterical phobias often lead to impotence which can in turn "bring about an anxiety neurosis just as the absence of external opportunity for adequate gratification can" by adding "and this in spite of the fact that the psychoneurotic symptoms themselves render possible a sort of disguised gratification and a certain relief of tension" (Jones, 1913).

7. Ferenczi is probably referring here to Freud's paper "Hysterische Phantasien und ihre Beziehung zur Bisexualität" ("Hysterical phantasies and their relation to bisexuality"), which appeared first in the *Zeitschrift für Sexualwissenschaft*, (*1*[1908]: 27–34), and then in *Sammlung kleiner Schriften zur Neurosenlehre 2* (pp. 138–145). Leipzig, Vienna: Deuticke, 1909, 2nd edn. 1912) (Freud, 1908a).
8. Again Jones followed Ferenczi's editorial suggestion: the phrase does not appear in the published version of Jones's paper: *Journal of Abnormal Psychology*, *8*(1913): 1–9.
9. Jones took Ferenczi's advice. In his paper he writes: "This conception can be related to Freud's view in which he traces the 'anxiety transformation of sexual hunger' to the fact that the ego deals with an internal danger in the same way that it is accustomed to deal with external dangers" (*Journal of Abnormal Psychology*, *8*(1913): p. 4). Jones had published a paper "On the nightmare" in *American Journal of Insanity* (Jones, 1910b).
10. Franz Deuticke (1850–1919), the publisher of the *Jahrbuch*, had also brought out *Studies on Hysteria*, *The Interpretation of Dreams*, *Sammlung kleiner Schriften zur Neurosenlehre* and *Schriften zur angewandten Seelenkunde*. The latter was taken over by Hugo Heller from Volume 3.
11. Hugo Heller (1870–1923), was a Viennese publisher and bookseller, a member of the Wednesday Society and an important link between psychoanalytic and literary circles in Vienna.
12. The "new Zentralblatt" was the *Zeitschrift*, published by Hugo Heller in Vienna.
13. Carl Gustav Jung (1875–1961), was a consultant at Zurich university psychiatric hospital, the "Burghölzli", and a promoter of Freud's work there. He was editor of the first psychoanalytic periodical, the *Jahrbuch für psychoanalytische und psychopathologische Forschungen*, which was published jointly by Freud and Bleuler. From 1910 until his split from Freud

in 1914, he served as the first President of the International Psychoanalytic Association. Ferenczi's critique of Jung's *Wandlungen und Symbole der Libido. Beiträge zur Entwicklungsgeschichte des Denkens* (*Psychology of the Unconscious: A Study of the Transformations and Symbolisms of the Libido: A Contribution to the History of the Evolution of Thought*) (Jung, 1912), which contained Jung's departure from Freud's libido theory, appeared as "Kritik der Jungschen *Wandlungen und Symbole der Libido*" (A critique of Jung's *Transformations and Symbolisms of the Libido*) (Ferenczi, 1913[124]).

4F

Budapest, 25 September 1913[1]

Dear Jones,[2]

I have been missing news from you for too long already,[3] and therefore want to approach you as an (in the first place, of course, interest-generating) agent of ferment, disturb your peace (death instinct) and force you to share with me once again some of the personal and other events, which concern our common interests. I feel this need all the more, because I have been almost without news since Munich,[4]—except for rather biased newspaper reports about the Adler Congress in Vienna.[5] Here in Budapest, a nonsensical, confused and malicious article, against Freud and for Adler, appeared in Pester Lloyd[6] to mark the occasion. The author (with whom I am not familiar) is Albert Ehrenstein,[7] whose name obviously does not oblige him in the slightest. It would be nice, and maybe effective, if you were to write a few lines to your friend J. Vészi,[8] editor-in-chief of P[ester] Ll[oyd], in connection with this and kindly ask him not to just print any old nonsense sent to him about ps[ycho]an[alysis]. It would be best, however, not to tell him the idea came from me; you might just say that he could turn to me for expert advice on such matters. If you write to him in a friendly manner, he will feel honored and flattered.—Perhaps I will spur Ignotus[9] into a response to this rubbish. (N.B. Ign[otus] talks about you a lot and would like to see you again soon. He numbers amongst the conquests you made in B[uda]pest).

In Munich, I spent another day with Prof. Freud (who was tired and depressed,[10] but from whom I have since received favorable news from Rome;[11] he is well and working), and a further day and a half with Lou Salomé who forced me to develop—that is to put down in writing the ideas about the death drive.[12] That seems to be her job. In B[uda]pest I found everything as it was. Dr. Lévy[13] is almost cured, but wants to work towards yet greater improvement when he returns from Vienna (Natural Science Congress).[14]

I still have few other patients, altogether 3–5 every day. It will soon be possible and necessary to discharge one pat[ient] (—the totem man [Totemmensch]—) as cured; he has become a different person without me having given him a single piece of advice or having found a single prospective dream in him. The new pat[ient] is a colossally difficult case of obsessional neurosis; I really have little hope there. (She has already made a serious suicide attempt).

I will return to you the letter f[rom] Putnam,[15] which I was given by Rank.[16] You have, no doubt, replied to him already; although you might perhaps tell him, should the occasion arise, that I consider just telepathy to be a possibility in this paper, while I look at prophecy only in as much as one can guess telepathically the future plans and wishes of others, for example.

I must, however, uphold most robustly the necessity of abstaining from moral advice during psychoanalysis. Should one be forced into it for external reasons, one must be sure that it is no longer Ψα one is engaged in. Thus, the question of "permission" for extramarital intercourse becomes irrelevant. The pat[ient] must have a feeling of complete independence and be able to make decisions about his personal relationships himself, but he also has to learn to take responsibility for them.

During the month of October, I will give two lectures.[17] 1.) On homosexuality, to the medical association (following the lecture in Weimar[18]), 2.) On psychoanalysis and the law,[19] in response to a request from the post-graduate training for public prosecutors and advocates. (About the latter, I have no idea as yet).

Please also write of your wife,[20] to whom I beg you to send my warmest regards.

Best wishes,
Ferenczi

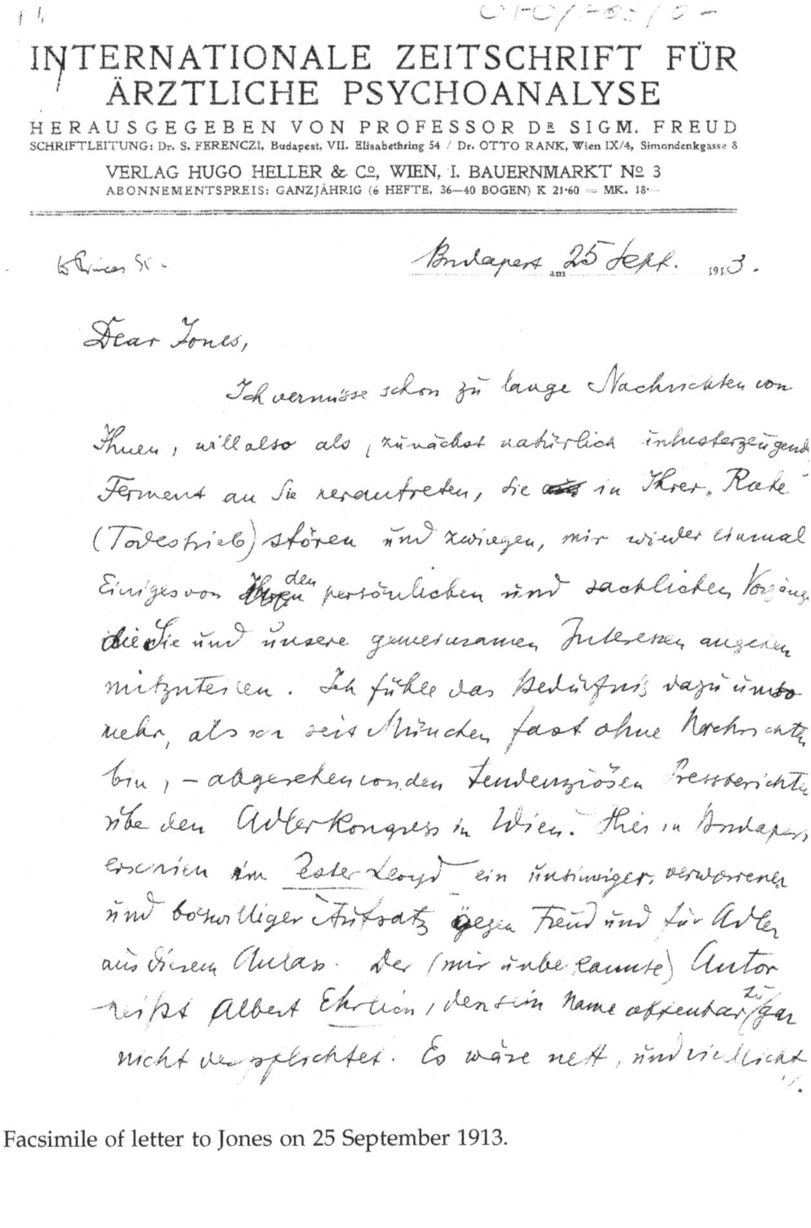

INTERNATIONALE ZEITSCHRIFT FÜR ÄRZTLICHE PSYCHOANALYSE
HERAUSGEGEBEN VON PROFESSOR Dr. SIGM. FREUD
SCHRIFTLEITUNG: Dr. S. FERENCZI, Budapest, VII. Elisabethring 54 / Dr. OTTO RANK, Wien IX/4, Simondenkgasse 8
VERLAG HUGO HELLER & Co., WIEN, I. BAUERNMARKT No 3
ABONNEMENTSPREIS: GANZJÄHRIG (6 HEFTE, 36—40 BOGEN) K 21·60 = MK. 18·—

Budapest, am 25 Sept. 1913.

Dear Jones,

Ich vermisse schon zu lange Nachrichten von Ihnen, will also als (zunächst natürlich unbewusst erzeugend) Ferment an Sie herantreten, die Sie in Ihrer Ruhe (Todestrieb) stören und zwingen, mir wieder einmal Einiges von den persönlichen und sachlichen Vorgängen, die Sie und unsere gemeinsamen Interessen angehen mitzuteilen. Ich fühle das Bedürfnis dazu umso mehr, als ich seit München fast ohne Nachrichten bin, – abgesehen von den tendenziösen Pressberichten über den Adler Kongress in Wien. Hier in Budapest erschien im Pester Lloyd ein unsinniger, verworrener und boshafter Aufsatz gegen Freud und für Adler aus diesem Anlass. Der (mir unbekannte) Autor heisst Albert Ehrlich, dessen Name offenbar zu gar nicht entspricht. Es wäre nett, und vielleicht ./.

Facsimile of letter to Jones on 25 September 1913.

Notes to letter 4F

1. Printed letterhead, hereafter: "INTERNATIONALE ZEITSCHRIFT FÜR ÄRZTLICHE PSYCHOANALYSE".
2. In English in the original.
3. Jones had been in analysis with Ferenczi for two sessions a day throughout June and July. He left Budapest on 1 August. Four days later, Ferenczi wrote to Freud that "I miss him *very much*. We have become intimate friends; I grew to love and treasure him; it was a pleasure to have such an intelligent, fine, and respectable pupil" (*Freud–Ferenczi, 1*, p. 503).
4. Since, that is, the Fourth International Psychoanalytic Congress in Munich from 5 to 9 September 1913.
5. When Adler seceded from the Vienna Society in 1912, he founded the Society of Free Analytic Research, renamed the Society for Individual Psychology later that year. In the following year he organised a Conference on emotional pathology in Vienna.
6. *Pester Lloyd* was a Budapest daily newspaper published in German (1854–1945).
7. The article was published in *Pester Lloyd* on 23 September 1913 under the title "Psychotherapeutenkongress" (Congress of psychotherapists). It was an account of the Wiener Kongress des Internationalen Vereins für medizinische Psychologie und Psychotherapie (Vienna Congress of the International Society for Medical Psychology and Psychotherapy), 19th and 20th September), where Adler lectured on the investigation of neuroses. Albert Ehrenstein (Vienna 1886–New York 1950) was a poet who later became a well-known figure in the German expressionist movement.
8. József Vészi (1858–1940) was from 1905 editor, and from 1909 to 1937 editor-in-chief, of *Pester Lloyd*. He also founded the daily newspaper *Budapesti Napló*, as well as the literary movement "Jung-Ungarn" (Young Hungary) and a journal of the same name. He came to be known as the "Nestor of Hungarian journalism". Jones would have become acquainted with him during his stay in Budapest in June and July.
9. Ignotus (Hugó Veigelsberg) (1869–1949) was a poet, journalist, and literary critic. From its creation in 1908 until 1926, he was editor-in-chief of the progressive literary journal *Nyugat* (Occident). He was a founding member of the Hungarian Psychoanalytic Association in 1913 and a translator as well as correspondent of Freud. He maintained a close friendship with Ferenczi (see Ferenczi's article "Ignotus, the understanding", 1924) in *Nyugat, 17*, no. 23), eventually writing his obituary (in: *Magyar Hírlap*, 28.5.1933 (see Ignotus, 1933)). After the fall of the 1919 Hungarian Republic of Councils, he moved to Vienna, but continued to

participate in literary life. In 1938, he emigrated to New York, returning to Budapest ten years later, already very ill.

10. Freud was low in the month before the Munich Congress, reporting to Ferenczi in early August that "I am unmistakably in a toxic condition similar to the one you saw me in last year . . . Always ruminating over the same dark thoughts, taking little things hard, aversion to food . . ." (*Freud–Ferenczi, 1*, pp. 504f). On top of this, the Congress was fraught as difficulties with Jung approached crisis point (see *Jones, 2*, pp. 101–103). It was, as Ferenczi put it to Freud, a "summer . . . really too full of disturbances to health!" (*Freud–Ferenczi, 1*, p. 508).
11. After the Munich Congress, Freud travelled to Rome, where he spent seventeen days in the company of Minna Bernays (*Freud–Ferenczi, 1*, pp. 506–509).
12. Lou Andreas Salomé (1861–1937) was a writer and psychoanalyst. Born in St Petersburg, she lived in Russia until aged twenty. As Ernest Jones observed, she had "a remarkable flair for great men". She first met Nietzsche in 1882, she married the orientalist Friedrich Carl Andreas (1846–1930) in 1886, had an affair with Rilke, and gravitated towards Freud. In 1911, she attended the Weimar Congress, by 1915 had opened a private practice in Göttingen, and in 1922 became a member of the Vienna Psychoanalytic Association. For Lou Andeas-Salomé's account of her meeting with Ferenczi, see *The Freud Journal* (Andreas-Salomé, 1964, pp. 170–172). She was interested in getting Ferenczi to expand on ideas in his "Entwicklungsstufen des Wirklichkeitssinnes" ("Stages in the development of the sense of reality") (Ferenczi, 1913[111]). Andreas-Salomé was interested in Ferenczi's "death instinct" as "proceeding from the original condition of the infant in the womb as the pleasurable condition of peace devoid of wishes" (Andreas-Salomé, 1964, p. 172; see also Avello, 1998).
13. Lajos Lévy (1875–1961) was a founder member of the Hungarian Psychoanalytic Association in 1913. He acted as General Practitioner to Ferenczi and the Róheim family, as well as being consultant and chief physician to several Budapest hospitals, and later Director of the Budapest Jewish hospital. Between 1917 and 1928 he edited the journal *Gyógyászat* (The Art of Healing), in which the first psychoanalytic papers published in Hungarian appeared. He emigrated to the UK in 1955 with his wife Kata Freund, sister of Anton von Freund and associate of Anna Freud. At Anna Freud's request, he wrote an important account of Ferenczi's final illness, undermining the charge that Jones and others made that Ferenczi became insane (see Bonomi, 1998).

14. The 85th congress of German natural scientists and physicians met in Vienna from 21 to 28 September 1913.
15. James Jackson Putnam (1846–1918) American neurologist and psychologist, was a professor at Harvard University, co-editor of the *Journal of Abnormal Psychology*, and founder and first president of the American Psychoanalytical Association (1911). In his letter dated 2 September 1913, Putnam wrote to Jones,

    > I was struck with one passage in Ferenczi's review, in which he seems, unless I strangely misread it, to endorse the *possibility* of a real prophetic power. This goes even beyond me, prepared as I am to admit the possibility of telepathy. (Hale, 1971, p. 278)

    The review in question was Ferenczi's (1913[124]) "Kritik der Jungschen *Wandlungen und Symbole der Libido*" (A critique of Jung's Transformations and Symbolisms of the Libido).
16. Otto Rank (1884–1939) introduced himself to Freud in the spring of 1905. He studied German and classical philology, obtaining a PhD in 1912. From 1906, he became the paid secretary and minute taker of the Viennese Wednesday Society, from 1912–1924, joint editor of *Imago*, and, from 1913, sole editor of the *Internationale Zeitschrift für (ärztliche) Psychoanalyse*. He headed international psychoanalytic publishing between 1914 and 1924. After the war, he worked in private practice. His book *Das Trauma der Geburt und seine Bedeutung für die Psychanalyse* (*The Trauma of Birth* (and its significance for psychoanalysis)) was published in 1924 in Leipzig, and the work he co-authored with Ferenczi, *Entwicklungsziele der Psychoanalyse: Zur Wechselbeziehung von Theorie und Praxis* (Developmental Goals of Psychoanalysis: On the Interrelationship of Theory and Practice; published in English as *The Development of Psychoanalysis* (1925)) (Ferenczi & Rank, 1924). Both were sources of heated controversy at the time. Rank went to Paris in 1924 and to the USA in 1934. On his split from the Freudian school, see Bókay, 1998; Leitner, 1998. See also Lieberman, 1984; Rudnytsky, 1991.
17. Most probably at the Budapest Royal Medical Association
18. The paper Ferenczi gave in Weimar (21–22 September 1911) was published under the title "Zur Nosologie der männlichen Homosexualität (Homoerotik)" ("On the nosology of male homosexuality (homoerotism)") (Ferenczi, 1914[136]).
19. Ferenczi gave his lecture "A pszichoanalízisről és annak jogi és társadalmi jelentőségéről" ("On psychoanalysis and its significance to society and the law") on 29 October 1913 to the national association of

judges and advocates. It was published in *Gyógyászat*, 8 February 1914 (Ferenczi, 1914).

20. Actually, Loe Kann (Louise Dorothea Kann) (?–1945), who was the rich daughter of a Dutch Jewish industrialist. Her brother founded the *Jewish Chronicle* Trust in London to assist those who wished to emigrate to Palestine. Their relationship started in 1906. They were not married officially, though they pretended to be a married couple, and went together to Toronto as man and wife. Freud, with whom she began analysis in June 1912, referred to her as Jones' wife (*Freud–Jones,* pp. 157, 159 *et passim*) and she signed herself "Loe Kann Jones" to Freud (letter, Freud Museum, 12 June 1912). Loe suffered from various somatic and psychic illnesses, including morphine addiction. Loe had already met her husband-to-be, Herbert Jones, a young American poet, by the end of 1912, and by the middle of May 1913 Freud referred to her as Ernest Jones' "former wife" (*Freud–Ferenczi, 1,* p. 488). She married Herbert on 1 June 1914 in Budapest, in the presence of Freud and Otto Rank as witnesses, and Ferenczi as interpreter (see Maddox, 2006, p. 47 *et passim*).

5F

INTERNATIONALE ZEITSCHRIFT FÜR
ÄRZTLICHE PSYCHOANALYSE

Budapest, 25 October 1913

Dear Friend,

Why have you remained silent so persistently? I hope you are not prevented by something which might disturb /internally or externally/ the relationship we have enjoyed thus far. Please put my mind at rest and let me know, too, whether you received my last letter (which I sent about three weeks ago).

And now a plea!

You are acquainted with my experiments, which concern psychical long-distance effects.—Now I finally have proof that my observations have been correct: a married couple[1] able to signal to each other without any of the means of communication we are familiar with. (The husband thinks of something |which I write down on a piece of paper|, is not allowed to say a word or ask anything and the wife |blindfolded| promptly guesses his thought |from a distance of 15 metres|. Controls of any kind permitted. It also yielded interesting links to psychoanalysis. (The guessing of the symbol instead of the actual etc. the role of sexuality.)

It is necessary for these things to be elaborated by our side first and not by the enemies of psychoanalysis, which is why I have decided to work both these and my earlier observations into a paper. I hope to have completed it in a few weeks.—

The couple are about to go to Vienna and then on to London. I should like to take this opportunity to present my findings (with a demonstration of the couple) to the "Psycho-med[ical] Society" and to the "Soc[iety] for Psych[ical] Res[earch]". A journey to London would be too much of a sacrifice, however, which is why I am asking whether you might be willing (and not afraid) to read my paper (on my behalf) in said societies; if that is not easily possible, would you know of someone who might do me this service?[2]

In any case, I shall give your address to the couple, so that you might convince yourself of the facts of the matter.

The "telepaths" are thinking of travelling to London in December or January.—

As far as my health is concerned, I am well. Yesterday, I wrote a rather sharp critique of Bleuler's Breslau paper[3]—I hope Prof. Freud will want to publish it. Every Sunday, I lecture to medical doctors.[4] Soon, I will submit my application for a professorship;[5] there is little hope. I have not been to Vienna yet.—

Write to me about everything concerning yourself.

Cordially yours,

Ferenczi

Notes to letter 5F

1. The couple referred to are "Professor" Alexander Roth and his wife. They appeared (unsuccessfully) with Ferenczi before the Vienna Society on 19 November when Ferenczi lectured on thought transference (*Minutes, 4,* p. 215; *Jones, 3,* p. 389) and later that month (23 November) they laid on a séance for Freud at his home, again unsuccessfully (*Freud–Ferenczi, 1,* pp. 523–525). It has proved impossible to trace "Professor Roth" or his wife.
2. Ferenczi became a member of the Society for Psychical Research in 1911 but Jones, unlike several contemporary British psychoanalysts, never joined. It is very unlikely that he would have agreed to present Ferenczi's paper. In any event it was not delivered to the Society for Psychical Research and there is no record of the Roths being involved with that Society. Ferenczi had not had much success with the Society. When in 1912 he had submitted his paper on "The psychoanalysis of suggestion and hypnosis" (Ferenczi, 1912[94]), it had met with "a polite rejection" on the grounds that "it was thought inadvisable [to publish it] in a lay publication because of the attitude of public opinion at that time to Freud and his work" (see in *Proceeding of the Society for Psychical Research,* Mitchell, 1938–1939, p. 183). With Ferenczi's consent it was passed on to the Psycho-Medical Society and published in 1912 in its *Transactions* (see *Freud–Ferenczi, 1*: p. 420).
3. Bleuler gave the opening paper, "Kritik der Freudschen Theorie" (A critique of Freudian theory) at the Congress of German psychiatrists that met in Breslau between 13 and 24 May 1913 (see Bleuler, 1913). The Congress was intended as a public statement from German psychiatrists about their suspicion of psychoanalysis. Bleuler had already quit the International Psychoanalytical Association, though he continued to support psychoanalysis. In his Breslau paper, he was even-handed towards psychoanalysis, taking issue with some parts of Freud's theory and finding value in others. Ferenczi's "sharp critique" appeared in the *Zeitschrift* (Ferenczi, 1914[150]). Freud wrote congratulating him on it as "precious and well deserved" on 26 October 1913 (*Freud–Ferenczi, 1,* p. 516). On the Breslau Congress, see Falzeder and Burnham, 2007.
4. Ferenczi refers here to a series of lectures he gave to medical students at the Medical Section of the Galileo Circle.
5. In November 1913, Ferenczi applied for a "Habilitation" (for a title of "Privatdozent") at the Medical Faculty of the Budapest University, with the theme "Pathology and treatment of the functional neuroses and psychoses". See Erős, 2011; see also more details below: 8F, note 4.

6F

INTERNATIONALE ZEITSCHRIFT FÜR
ÄRZTLICHE PSYCHOANALYSE

Vienna, 2 November 1913.[1]

Dear Friend,

I am writing at Prof. Freud's desk because what I have to tell you does not brook any delay. For the same reason, I will leave your personal news unanswered this time.

Now listen:

Prof. Freud recently wrote a reply to Maeder,[2] in which he expressed his doubts about Jung's bona fides. Following this, a letter from Jung arrived within the last few days, in which he—referring to Freud's comments—resigned as editor of the Jahrbuch.[3]—Concerning this matter, we held a meeting of the Committee today (Prof. Freud, Sachs,[4] Rank, Heller a[nd] myself). We agreed that Prof. Freud should just acknowledge J[ung]'s resignation a[nd] transfer the ed[itorship] to Hitschmann[5] a[nd] Abraham.[6] The Jahrbuch is then to appear once a year as a slimmer volume (15–18 spreads) and will contain, alongside original articles which are important in principle, a detailed literary critique of the Ψα year. Whether this plan will come to fruition is, for the time being, dependent as well, still, on the behaviour of Prof. Bleuler and that of Deuticke.[7]

Prof. Freud also used the occasion to raise the issue of whether the time might not have come, to dissolve the last remaining connection with Zurich too: the I[nternational] Ps[ycho]A[nalytic] Association. We declared in favour unanimously.—As to how this might be achieved, we reached the following conclusion: four local groups (Vienna, Berlin Budapest and the large American group) will jointly make an application |:N.B. the numerical majority of the I[nternational] Ps[ycho]A[nalytic] A[ssociation]| to the president of the Association, to the effect that it should be dissolved. Vienna, Berlin and B[uda]pest would easily be won over to this; where the American group is concerned, we have to turn to you for information and for the relaying of the plans for the operation.[8]—You should write immediately to the leading personalities in America and obtain their agreement to this step. You might let them know that co-operation with J[ung] is no longer possible and that a new Association is to be founded, for the time being with Freud as president and Dr. Jones as vice-president, which the groups would be able to join soon.

Please be so kind and let Prof. Freud have your views on this matter by return of post. We ask you to take into consideration that a withdrawal - which would be inevitable otherwise - would be more detrimental than dissolution because in that instance, Jung would stay in power and president, while we become the outcasts. Write too, whether you are of the view that we should wait for a response from the Americans, or whether we should start the operation independently of them. Also tell us something about the prospects with regards to the New York group.

In any case, reply at once and take the necessary steps without delay because the matter is most urgent.

I am departing for B[uda]pest tonight and hope to receive a postcard from you as well.

Warm regards,

Your devoted friend
S. Ferenczi

Of course the operation is, for the time being, strictly a Committee secret.

Notes to letter 6F

1. This letter is also published (Wittenberger, 1995, pp. 116–117; Wittenberger & Tögel, 1999, pp. 32–34).
2. Alphonse Maeder (1882–1971), a Swiss psychotherapist, was temporarily President of the Zurich Association. He worked at the Bellevue clinic in Kreuzlingen for a short time in 1910 and while there began corresponding with Freud. He followed Jung after his split from Freud.
3. Jung wrote to Freud on 27 October saying that he had heard from Maeder that Freud doubted his *bona fides*, and that he was therefore resigning from the editorship of the *Jahrbuch* (see *Freud–Jung*, p. 550).
4. Hanns Sachs (1881–1947) trained as a lawyer and was a member of the Vienna Association from October 1910. One of the first to be interested in the application of psychoanalysis to the humanities, he, with Rank, initiated the publication of the journal *Imago*. He was a founding member of the "Secret Committee" in 1912 and became the Berlin Institute's first professional lay analyst (1920–1932). In 1932, he emigrated to Boston in the USA. There, he co-founded *American Imago* in 1939.
5. Eduard Hitschmann (1871–1957) was a member of the Wednesday Society from 1905. His book *Freuds Neurosenlehre nach ihrem gegenwärtigen Stande* (*Freud's Theories of the Neuroses*) (1911), was the first systematic exposition of psychoanalysis. In 1922, he became the first head of the Vienna Clinic of Psychoanalysis. He emigrated to England in 1938 and to Boston in the USA in 1940.
6. Karl Abraham (1877–1925) was a German psychiatrist who worked with Jung and Bleuler at the Burghölzli from 1904. He was in very close contact with Freud from 1907 onwards. From 1908 until his death, he was President of the Berlin Psychoanalytic Association. A founding member of the "Secret Committee" in 1912, he took over from Jung as President of the International Psychoanalytic Association in 1914, occupying this position until 1918 and being re-elected in 1924. He fell ill with septic pneumonia in 1925.
7. Jung had edited the *Jahrbuch* with Bleuler as Editor-in-Chief. With Jung's resignation from the International Psychoanalytical Association, Ferenczi seems to have been worried that Jung might "get the Jahrbuch" (*Freud–Ferenczi, 1*, p. 517) and that Deuticke had a key role in ensuring that it passed into Freud's hands. Freud wrote to Ferenczi on 4 November 1913 that "the situation with Deuticke is bad", but, by 9 November, he informed Ferenczi that "Deuticke has become aware of his hastiness and has definitively come to terms with me" (*Freud–Ferenczi, 1*, pp. 517, 520). Concerns remained, however, about him (see Jones's letter to Freud, 29

November 1913 (*Freud–Jones*, pp. 244–245)). The sixth and last volume of the *Jahrbuch* was finally brought out by Deuticke (1914) under the slightly amended title of *Jahrbuch der Psychoanalyse. Neue Folge des Jahrbuchs für psychoanalytische und psychopathologische Forschungen*, with Freud as sole publisher and Abraham and Hitschmann as editors. Since Bleuler was Editor-in-Chief of the *Jahrbuch*, Freud also had to persuade him to step down. Bleuler's replacement by Freud and the appointment of Abraham and Hitschmann as editors was announced in the *Jahrbuch*, *5*(1913): 757.

8. Although the London Psycho-Analytical Society had been founded with Jones as President only days before Ferenczi's letter, on 30 October, it was not yet a component society of the International Association.

7F

INTERNATIONALE ZEITSCHRIFT FÜR ÄRZTLICHE PSYCHOANALYSE

Budapest, 8 November 1913

Dear Friend,

Herewith a letter f[rom] Abraham,[1] which you might be kind enough to return to Prof. F[reud]. I have read your letter to Fr[eud],[2] but was convinced by it only in as far as I consider the dissolution impossible to carry out. The withdrawal, however, of Freud, Jones, Abraham, Sachs, Rank, those from Budapest,[3] Brill,[4] Putnam etc cannot be put off. We must not give the Zurich lot time to take cover behind Freud's name and thus gain strength. The world should know of Jung's break [with Freud].[5] After all, one will find true "psychoanalysis" where Freud is himself.

Am in a hurry, will therefore end and send my most cordial regards. I will sort out the telepathic matter with the Soc[iety] for Psych[ical] Res[earch]. Next week, I will demonstrate the telep[athy] experiments at the Vienna Psychoanal[tic] Association.[6]

Cordially,

Ferenczi

Kind regards to Mrs Lou.
I thought she would be in Vienna by now![7]

Notes to letter 7F

1. This is probably Abraham's letter to Freud from 4 November 1913 agreeing to take on the editing of the *Jahrbuch* and setting out his thoughts about the future of the International Psychoanalytical Association in relation to Jung (*Freud–Abraham*, pp. 205–206). Jones returned it to Freud with his letter of 11 November 1913 (*Freud–Jones*, p. 237).
2. Probably Jones's letter of 4 November 1913 (*Freud–Jones*, pp. 234–236) in which he discusses with Freud the news and proposals made in Ferenczi's letter of 2 November.
3. Besides Ferenczi (President), the members of the Budapest group, founded on 19 May 1913, included István Hollós (deputy President), Lajos Lévy (Treasurer), Sándor Radó (Secretary), and Ignotus (the only ordinary member).
4. Abraham Arden Brill (1874–1948), psychiatrist, was born in Galicia (then Austria-Hungary). He emigrated on his own to New York in 1889, completing his medical studies there in 1903. After a year-long internship at the Burghölzli and a short analysis with Freud, he returned to the United States in 1908, where he founded the New York Psychoanalytic Society, whose first President he became. He was also Professor of Psychiatry at New York University College and lecturer in psychoanalysis at Columbia University. From 1929 to 1936, he became the first President of the reorganised American Psychoanalytic Association. Brill is also important as one of the early translators of Freud.
5. Jung finally resigned the presidency of the International Psychoanalytic Association in April 1914. On 20 April 1914, he wrote to Freud,

   > Dear Mr. President, The latest developments have convinced me that my views are in such sharp contrast to the views of the majority of members of our Association, that I can longer consider myself a suitable personality to be president. I therefore tender my resignation to the council of the presidents of the branch societies, with many thanks for the confidence I have enjoyed hitherto. Very truly yours, Dr. C. G. Jung. (*Freud–Jung*, p. 551)

6. Ferenczi spoke on "Experiments with thought-transference" to the Vienna Society on 19 November 1913. Freud attended (*Minutes*, 4, p. 211). The minutes of the meeting are missing, but on 29 November 1913, Ferenczi enclosed his own account of the meeting in a letter to Freud:

   > On November 19, Dr S. Ferenczi from Budapest gave a lecture in the Vienna Society on thought transference, in which he shared his

> experiences on the subject—which were gained by chance and collected in an experimental manner. He does not consider these experiences conclusive evidence, but he demonstrates a married couple, who, in his opinion, do seem to settle the question of telepathy in a positive sense. The experiments, which were carried out under the observation of members of the Society and later repeated, yielded a positive result in only a few instances, so they were not sufficient to convince members of the Society of the actuality of thought transference. (*Freud–Ferenczi, 1*, pp. 523–525)

Freud was not impressed when Roth and his wife conducted a séance at Berggasse 19 four days later, on 23 November 1913. Neither was Anna Freud, who wrote to Jones, "I remember that both my father and I were taken aback by the rough way in which the poor woman was urged, forced and hustled to produce results" (*Jones, 3*, p. 416).

7. Loe Kann travelled to Vienna on 28 November (*Freud–Jones*, p. 244), to continue her analysis with Freud (on Kann, see letter 4F, note 20).

8F

16. December 1913

Dear Friend,

Just a few quick lines to make sure you receive them before your departure.[1]—First of all: your idea is <u>excellent</u>, I think it is the best you have had so far. Your old problem ("social instincts"),[2] which always reminded me a little too much of the "prospective tendency", is resolving itself more and more in the concepts of ego and sex[uality].[3]

<u>Individuals</u> a[nd] smaller groups are <u>in fact</u> already in the genital phase of socialism (object love), while larger groups remain stuck in the sadistic phase (war).

My lectureship is finished in the negative sense.[4] Jendrassik[5] pulled out all the stops to ensure my downfall and he succeeded.

I certainly hope to see you in Vienna or B[uda]pest. Perhaps over Christmas, I will have my nose repaired in Vienna after all.

Everything else in person.[6]

Kind regards

Ferenczi

Notes to letter 8F

1. Jones left for Vienna on 19 December.
2. Jones hypothesised the existence of a "herd instinct" or "social instinct", based on the works of Gustave Le Bon, William McDougall, Wilfred Trotter and others. See, for example, Jones, 1924c; *Freud–Jones*, p. 372.
3. Ferenczi is probably warning Jones that his thinking is reminiscent of Jung's (though the notion of the "prospective tendency" is not confined to Jung's work). The concept of a "prospective tendency" was topical. Maeder had published a paper in 1912 in which he had advanced the idea ("Über die Funktion des Traumes" (On the function of dreams), Maeder, 1912), and in 1911 Adler had argued that dreams involved "thinking ahead" ("Beitrag zur Lehre vom Widerstand") (Contribution to the theory of resistance), Adler, 1911). In a letter to Freud on 2 April 1914 complimenting him on his paper "On narcissism" (Freud, 1914c), Abraham commented,

   > Your expositions about the ego-ideal are especially valuable for practical purposes. . . . In particular, the distinction between ego-ideal and true sublimation. . . . I think this is where the contrast between Jung's therapy and Ψα can be most pointedly stressed. The 'life task' and all similar concepts (including the prospective tendency of the unconscious) are in fact nothing but an appeal to the ego-ideal and thereby a path that by-passes all real possibilities of sublimation (with the unconscious intention of avoiding them). (*Freud–Abraham*, p. 226)

   In 1914 Freud added a footnote to *The Interpretation of Dreams* critical of Maeder and Adler's views (Freud, 1900a, p. 579).
4. Ferenczi's application for "Habilitation" was strongly supported by the professor of neurology Ernő Emil Moravcsik, but was refused by the majority of the council of the Medical Faculty on 25 November 1913, led by Professor Ernő Jendrassik (see below). In 1918 and 1919, Ferenczi continued his efforts for a university appointment. His efforts were supported by petitions of medical students and by Freud himself, who wrote an article on the teaching of psychoanalysis in universities, which was first published in Hungarian translation (Freud, 1919j; Schröter, 2009). In March 1919, Ferenczi's application was rejected again by the faculty council, based on Professor Jendrassik's negative opinion. However, Ferenczi was appointed to a chair of psychoanalysis on 25 April 1919, by the government of the Hungarian Republic of Councils (see Erős, 2011; Giampieri & Erős, 1987).

5. Ernő Jendrassik (1858–1921) studied under Charcot in Paris during 1885, became a lecturer in 1887, professor of neuropathology within the medical faculty of Budapest university in 1903, professor of internal medicine in 1908, and a member of the Hungarian Academy of Sciences in 1898.
6. Ferenczi wrote to Freud on 10 December 1913 that

> I think I have finally succeeded in discovering the *real* source of my sleep disturbances in the relative insufficiency of my nasal breathing. So I will probably have to go to Vienna at Christmas to take care of this matter. (*Freud–Ferenczi, 1*, p. 526)

He planned to travel to Vienna on 21 December, to see Jones when he arrived (*Freud–Jones*, p. 250) to give him the rest of his news "in person", and to meet with Freud. In the event, he postponed his trip because he had to go to Vienna on 25 December for the operation on his nose (*Freud–Ferenczi, 1*, p. 528). Freud travelled to Hamburg, where he planned to meet Abraham, on 24 December (*Freud–Ferenczi, 1*, p. 527).

Ernő Jendrassik (1858–1921).

Ernő Emil Moravcsik (1858–1924).

9F

INTERNATIONALE ZEITSCHRIFT FÜR
ÄRZTLICHE PSYCHOANALYSE

Budapest, 16 March 1914

Dear Friend,

You know me and hence know that where I am concerned, a period of silence does not signify anything dangerous. Although this time, my[1] silence really has gone on a little too long, thus—I am quite worried now not to have heard from you for so long. And I write just to provoke a reply from you, really, because I have nothing new to tell about myself. Everything is as it was: practice almost full, much work planned, dilatoriness in its execution, neurasthenic insomnia but otherwise in pretty satisfactory health. Have been to Vienna less frequently because the Zeitschrift did not come out for so long, but want to go and see Freud—the newest grandfather—next Sunday |:Mrs Sophie, the second daughter, was delivered ["genesen"] of a girl,[2] as we put it in German.[3]—The publication of the 3rd collection of my Hungarian ps[ycho]-an[alytic] essays[4] caused quite a stir; the newspapers did some advertising for me.

Budapest is as always: full of enthusiasm for anything interesting, but without the stamina for hard work. I am beginning to think that I myself am of the Typus Budapestiensis.

I think of you often and am sorry that we cannot chat to one another every day. Indeed, talking with you was so stimulating, that I have been looking for a substitute ever since, but quite in vain. Ignotus is busy with a thousand other things, little Radó[5] is an intelligent chap, but very young still and essentially of a just critical disposition. It is true that in Dr. Hollós[6] (consultant to the lunatic asylum in Nagyszeben) I have found a talented psychoanalyst, although he lives much too far away from here and his ambition complex irritates me now and then—perhaps because it collides with my own!

Please write to me soon and forgive my laziness.

Kindest regards,

Ferenczi

P.S.: I consider Abraham's suggestion to be premature. We should wait and see what impact the Jahrbuch (Freud's "History of Ψα")[7] will have before taking action.[8]

Notes to letter 9F

1. Corrected in the original from "the".
2. Ferenczi is mistaken here: Freud's first grandchild, born on 11 March 1914, actually was a boy, Ernst Wolfgang Halberstadt, whom Freud observed playing the "fort-da" game. Ernst later became a psychoanalyst.
3. In German, "genesen" also means "to recuperate/to convalesce".
4. *Ideges tünetek keletkezése és eltűnése és egyéb értekezések a pszichoanalízis köréből* [Origin and disappearance of Neurotic Symptoms, and other treatises on Psycho-Analysis] (Ferenczi, 1914[149])
5. Sándor Radó (1890–1972), a Hungarian physician and psychoanalyst who studied law in Budapest, medicine in Berlin, and obtained his doctorate in Budapest in 1915. He was a founding member and secretary of the Hungarian Psychoanalytic Association in 1913. During the Hungarian Councils' Republic in 1919, he was ordered to service at the Department of Higher Education, People's Commissariat for Public Education. In this position, he was influential in Ferenczi's appointment to professorship. He emigrated to Berlin in 1922, where he went into analysis with Abraham and became one of the teachers at the Berlin Psychoanalytic Institute. In 1931, he emigrated to the USA. During his exile in New York, he founded several centres for psychoanalytic training and research. From 1944 until his retirement in 1955, he was director of Columbia University's Institute of Psychiatry. Owing to his fundamentally organic orientation, he increasingly distanced himself from Freud, leaving the New York Association in 1944 and, with Carl Binger, Abram Kardiner, and others, founded a separate analytic institute at Columbia University, which was recognised by the American Psychoanalytic Association. Radó left a considerable mark on institutional structures as well as on subsequent generations of analysts (Tomlison, 2010).
6. István Hollós (1872–1957), Hungarian psychiatrist and psychoanalyst who was a friend and collaborator of Ferenczi. He worked as a psychiatrist in Nagykálló, Nagyszeben, and at the Angyalföld hospital in Budapest. From 1900–1909, he was physician and, from 1919–1925, chief physician, at the state hospital for mentally insane "Lipótmező" in Budapest. A founding member of the Hungarian Psychoanalytic Association in 1913, he translated *The Interpretation of Dreams*, was analysed by Freud during 1918, and later had a training analysis with Paul Federn. He was a pioneer of the application of psychoanalytic methods in psychiatry and of the open-door system of psychiatric treatment. Due probably to his Jewish descent, he was forced to retire in 1925. With Ferenczi, he published *Zur Psychoanalyse der paralytischen Geistesstörungen*

(*Psychoanalysis and the Psychic Disorders of General Paresis*) (Ferenczi & Hollós, 1922[239]). 1927 saw the publication of his book under the original title *Búcsúm a sárga háztól. Dr. Pfeiflein különös írása az elmebetegek felszabadításáról* (Behind the yellow wall: Dr. Telemach Pfeiflein's peculiar writing on the liberation of the lunatic) (Hollós, 1927). After Ferenczi's death, he became President of the Hungarian Psychoanalytic Association. He published several works on the psychoanalysis of language and vocalisation. In 1944, the Swedish diplomat Raoul Wallenberg saved him and his wife from being shot by Hungarian Fascist gangs on the banks of the Danube (see his letter to Paul Federn, dated 17 February 1946: "Brief eines Entronnenen" (Letter of an escapee), Hollós, 1974).

7. "Zur Geschichte der psychoanalytischen Bewegung" ("On the history of the psycho-analytic movement") (Freud, 1914d).
8. Abraham had recently sent a circular letter to members of the Committee setting out plans to break with Jung in May. The circular letter is printed in *Freud–Abraham*, pp. 221–222.

István Hollós(1872–1957).

Sándor Radó (1890–1972).

10F

Prof Ernest Jones
69 Portland Court
London W.

Brioni, 11 April 1914[1]

Dear Jones,

Since yesterday we have been busy exploring the island of Brioni near Pola [Pula].[2] Science is taking a rest. In this heavenly landscape there is nothing to disturb our calm. We are very well. The weather is marvellous.

	Ferenczi
Greetings	Rank
	Freud[3]

Notes to letter 10F

1. Picture postcard in Ferenczi's hand.
2. Jones provides the history of this trip to Brioni:

> Freud had invited Ferenczi to repeat their pleasant sojourn in Arbe (today: the island of Rab in Croatia) of the previous year and suggested bringing his daughter Anna along with him. She had been running a temperature for some time and he was anxious about her. Brioni was then chosen as being more accessible (from Pola). At the last moment Anna was found to have whooping cough, so Freud took Rank with him instead. They left Vienna on the evening of April 9 and got back on April 13, a long journey for a taste of sea air. (*Jones*, 2, p. 118)

3. Each man signed his own name and Rank sent greetings.

11F

INTERNATIONALE ZEITSCHRIFT FÜR
ÄRZTLICHE PSYCHOANALYSE

Budapest, 20 May 1914

Dear Friend,[1]

At last, I want to let you know I am still alive, although I do not really have anything important to tell you. Just to stimulate a reply, however, even a letter without content will do.

How are you? How is your practice going? How are the scientific (Ψα) conditions shaping up in England? Did the break with Zurich have any after-effects in the London group?[2]—and how about America? How is your health? (Physically and mentally). What are you working on? And there are another hundred questions I should like to have you answer.—What I can offer you in return is precious little: Physically, I am much better now; (another correction to the nose will be necessary), practice going well. Hungarian Ps[ycho]A[nalysis] is always a central preoccupation (lately, Adlerian tendencies have announced themselves).[3] Two new members have been admitted: the physician Dr. J. Hárnik[4] (a diligent but difficult to treat chap due to personal complexes, our future Adler perhaps*) a[nd] Dr. G. Szilágyi[5] (doctor at law, ex-patient, journalist).

I have not done much lately, except for some notes on drive theory, which I aim to put together soon(?).

I have, I believe, always accepted your suggestions regarding the English translation. Did you talk to M. Prince[6] about this?

Your portrait is a splendid success. I thank you for that; gradually, I too will come to own a complete gallery of Committee members.[7]

Kindest regards,

Ferenczi

*(but much less astute and craven)[8]

Notes to letter 11F

1. In English in the original.
2. Jones had brought together colleagues to found the London Psycho-Analytical Society on 30 October 1913. Three of the founding members, David Eder (Secretary of the Society), Constance Long, and Maurice Nicoll, were influenced by Jung, making the "break with Zurich" problematic. In 1919, after a hiatus during the war, Jones dissolved the London Society and reformed it as the British Psycho-Analytical Society, "expel[ling] the Jung 'rump'" (*Freud–Jones*, p. 328). Eder rejoined the Freudian ranks of the British Society after analysis with Ferenczi in 1923.
3. A year earlier, Ferenczi had written to Freud about "a *Dr. Varjas*, a high school teacher, who is interested in psychoanalysis. . . . He is an *Adlerian*; he recently wrote a shabby Hungarian *Interpretation of Dreams* . . ." (*Freud–Ferenczi, 1*, p. 479). Sándor Varjas (1885–1940) was a teacher and philosopher, member of the Hungarian Psychoanalytic Association in 1918. He played an active role in the Councils' Republic; afterwards he was sentenced to long imprisonment, but, in 1922, was allowed to leave for Russia in the framework of a prisoners exchange agreement with the Soviet government. He became a professor of philosophy at the Moscow University. He fell victim to Stalin's purges.
4. Jenő Hárnik (189?–1937), Hungarian physician and psychoanalyst, received his medical degree in 1919, and was an early Ferenczi pupil, acting as his assistant at the university clinic during 1919. He was an active member of the Galileo Circle, a hotbed of young, progressive, left-wing intellectuals, founded on 22 November 1908 mostly by medical students. Hárnik participated in the drawing up of reforms for state hospitals in 1919. In 1922, he emigrated to Berlin and became a member of the Berlin Psychoanalytic Association and then, in 1933, emigrated to Denmark, where he played a role in the organisation of the Danish psychoanalytic movement.
5. Géza Szilágyi (1875–1958), became an LLD in 1919 with a doctoral thesis on anarchism, but first and foremost he was a poet and publicist. Analysed by Ferenczi, he joined the Hungarian Psychoanalytic Association in 1914. In addition to numerous poems, novels, and dramas, he published various psychoanalytic essays.
6. Morton Prince (1854–1929), was a Harvard-trained neurologist and psychiatrist and professor in Boston. In 1906, he founded the *Journal of Abnormal Psychology* and remained its publisher until his death. Between 1898 and 1911 he worked on dissociative phenomena, publishing his famous case of Sally Beauchamp, a study in multiple personality in 1906. Jones,

himself a neurologist, stayed with Prince at his home in Boston and met his Harvard group towards the end of 1908, having moved to Toronto in September. Prince made him assistant editor of his *Journal*. Prince was sceptical about Freud's theory of the origin of the neuroses and, by 1911, relations had cooled with Jones. Nevertheless, in 1913, on 22 July, Jones wrote to Freud that he was

> going to translate eleven of Ferenczi's papers (1916[186]), to make a book for Prince's Monograph Series. At present we are in the middle of some New York chicanerie on the matter, in which as usual Jelliffe is involved. F. has cabled to stop them. (*Freud–Jones*, p. 213)

Jones seems to have confused Jelliffe's *Journal of Nervous and Mental Disease* Monograph Series with Prince's publishing interests. Whatever the chicanerie, the translation of Ferenczi's papers, fifteen not eleven, appeared under the imprint of Richard G. Badger in Boston, the publisher for Prince's *Journal of Abnormal Psychology*. The Monograph Series would eventually publish Ferenczi and Hollós's *Psycho-Analysis and the Psychic Disorder of General Paresis* (1922) and Ferenczi and Rank's *The Development of Psychoanalysis* (1925).

7. It might be a photograph made by Max Halberstadt (1914), or a drawing by Hermann Struck (1914).
8. Inserted by Ferenczi.

12F

Budapest, 20 May 1914

Ungarische Psychoanalytische Vereinigung.
Verbandsverein der Internationalen Psychoanalytischen Vereinigung.
Univ. Prof. Dr. Ernest Jones

69 Portland Court
London.[1]

Esteemed Professor![2]

We are honoured to share with you the following excerpt from the minutes of the Annual General Meeting of the Hungarian Psychoanalytic Association, which took place on 16.V.1914:

"The President recalls warmly the pleasant relations, which developed during the summer of 1913 between the members of the Association and the current president of the London Group, Prof. Dr. Ernest Jones, who was in Budapest for an extended stay. In view of the great service Prof. Jones has done psychoanalysis, the President proposes to elect Prof. Dr. Ernest Jones an Honorary Member of the Association. The Annual General Meeting unanimously accepts the President's motion."

We are pleased to be able to bring this resolution of the Association to your attention.

Yours faithfully,
Budapest, 20th May 1914.

The Board of the Hungarian
Psychoanalytic Association

Dr. Alex. Radó
Secretary

Dr. S. Ferenczi
President

Notes to letter 12F

1. The original is typewritten except for the signatures.
2. Jones had been made Professor in Toronto in 1911, much to Freud's delight, because the title helped to confer respectability on psychoanalysis, though at the time allegations against Jones for sexual misconduct were in danger of bringing it into disrepute (see Maddox, 2006, pp. 90–99).

CFC/F03/15

Ungarische Psychoanalytische Vereinigung.
Verbandsverein der Internationalen Psychoanalytischen Vereinigung.

Herrn Univ. Prof. Dr. Ernest Jones

69 Portland Court
L O N D O N .

Hochverehrter Herr Professor!

Wir beehren uns Ihnen folgenden Auszug aus dem Protokoll der Generalversammlung vom 19. V. 1914. der Ungarischen Psychoanalytischen Vereinigung mitzuteilen:

"Präsident gedenkt in warmen Worten der angenehmen Beziehungen, die sich im Sommer 1913 zwischen den Mitgliedern der Vereinigung und dem d.z. Obmann der Ortsgruppe London, Herrn Prof. Dr. Ernest Jones, der sich längere Zeit in Budapest aufhielt, entwickelten. In Hinsicht auf die grossen Verdienste, die sich Prof. Jones um die Psychoanalyse erworben hat, schlägt Präsident vor, Herrn Prof. Dr. Ernest Jones zum Ehrenmitglied der Vereinigung zu wählen. Die Generalversammlung nimmt den Vorschlag des Präsidenten einstimmig an."

Wir freuen uns, diesen Beschluss der Vereinigung Ihnen zur Kenntnis bringen zu können.

Mit vorzüglicher Hochachtung
Budapest, 20. Mai 1914.

der Vorstand der Ungarischen Psychoanalytischen Vereinigung:

MAGYARORSZÁGI PSYCHOANALITIKAI EGYESÜLET 1913.

Dr. Alex. Radó
Sekretär.

Dr S. Ferenczi
Präsident.

Letter to Jones on the honorary membership of the Hungarian Psychoanalytic Association.

13F

INTERNATIONALE ZEITSCHRIFT FÜR
ÄRZTLICHE PSYCHOANALYSE

Budapest, 23 June 1914

Dear Friend,

In order to pay respect at least belatedly, I am forced to forego answering your questions this time (!), since I mislaid your letter,—maybe to bring about just this kind of situation, despite your reminder/warning.[1]—I have quite a lot to tell you, however. I will start immediately with the (for me) most important matter: notwithstanding the long tradition of spending the summer vacation with the Freuds, I recently wrote to Freud that maybe this time, I should make an exception from the rule and leave him completely to himself and his family. He responded with agreement, particularly since he is planning to spend the best part of his holidays in Tyrol writing his entry for Krauss's Encyclopedia,[2] and because it is easiest to do such work alone. Hence, I can arrange my vacation—from August 1st to about September 5th—as I please, and my first idea was to offer myself as a summer companion to yourself. I was thinking of some time in London, or maybe in

Paris, but then also a trip round France or England. And I could still call on Freud in Tyrol—for a day or two—on the return journey.[3]—What do you think? How does this fit with your plans for the summer? I hope you will answer me just as frankly and freely as Freud.—Should you agree with my suggestion in principle, please do feel completely at liberty regarding dates; you are the one who is familiar with local[4] conditions and will thus have to make the Cicerone, so to speak!

Apart from that, just a few small bits of news: you already know about Freud and the Jones couple's sojourn in Budapest.[5] Ignotus too is legally divorced from his wife already. With me, everything is as before, many projects, a few serviceable ideas as well, which I can share with you. (One could also get down to work for a week or two, somewhere on the coast, for example?!) Freud a[nd] Abraham asked me to give a paper on "The Tasks and Aims of the I[nternational] Ps[ychoanalytic] A[ssociation]" at the congress.[6] The occultists are meeting in Berlin from 16th – 24th Oct.,[7] perhaps we will make a trip there from our own congress.

Kind regards from Your ["Ihrem"]
—or better your ["Deinem"][8]

Ferenczi

Notes to letter 13F

1. The German "Mahnung", used by Ferenczi in the original, can mean either reminder or warning.
2. Friedrich Krauss (1858–1936), professor at the University of Graz and a director at the Charité Hospital in Berlin, had approached Freud in 1912 to contribute to the encyclopaedia, but negotiations with Krauss and his co-editor, Theodor Brugsch, were fraught with difficulties. In November 1913, they agreed that he would write "A psychoanalytic account of the neuroses", but no sooner did he begin work on it the following summer than war broke out. Although the editors renewed their request to Freud after the war, there was no psychoanalytic contribution to Krauss's *Spezielle Pathologie und Therapie innerer Krankheiten* (Special pathology and therapy of internal diseases), twelve volumes (Krauss & Brugsch, 1919–1928) (see *Jones, 2,* pp. 248–249).
3. Jones welcomed Ferenczi's suggestion (*Freud–Jones,* p. 288) but the war put paid to these holiday plans. On 28 June 1914, the Serbian student, Gavrilo Princip, assassinated the heir to the throne of the Austro-Hungarian monarchy, Franz Ferdinand, and his wife in Sarajevo. On 28 July 1914, Austria-Hungary declared war on Serbia, mobilising on 31 July 1914.
4. "Local" was inserted later.
5. The "Jones couple" are Loe Kann and Herbert Jones. At the beginning of June 1914, Freud and Rank travelled to Budapest for their wedding, to act along with Ferenczi as witnesses (see Freud's telegram to Ferenczi dated 24 May1914 (*Freud–Ferenczi, 1,* p. 555)).
6. An international psychoanalytic congress was planned to take place in Dresden on 20 and 21 September 1914. It did not happen because of the war.
7. This meeting was also cancelled due to the war. In a letter written the day after this letter, Freud urged Ferenczi to take part (*Freud–Ferenczi, 1,* pp. 559–560).
8. German distinguishes between a formal (*Ihrem*) and an informal, personal (*Deinem*) address; in all subsequent letters, Ferenczi uses the informal address.

14F

INTERNATIONALE ZEITSCHRIFT FÜR
ÄRZTLICHE PSYCHOANALYSE

Budapest, 20 July 1913 [1914][1]

Dear Jones,

Well then: agreed; I will come to London and accept your hospitality.[2] I shall come quite without an itinerary and just know very generally that I will spend most of the time in London and with you. I am able to tolerate being alone for longer periods only with difficulty and thus will have to burden you (at least during your spare time). I shall, however, bring writing paper; perhaps your diligence will prove infectious and make me decide, finally, to commit to paper some of the things which have preoccupied me. However, by way of recompense for all of this trouble, you must accept, at the very least, that while I am there we continue with the training analysis you began with me here. I am thinking of proper analytic sessions.

I do not know yet when I will arrive in London; during the first week of August in any case.

The approaching reunion makes it unnecessary to tell you other things by letter.

Herewith a circular[3] from Abraham. Please send it back to Berlin (with your comments).—

Till we meet again, happily quite soon,

Yours truly,

Ferenczi

Notes to letter 14F

1. Ferenczi must have made a mistake writing the date. The letter could only have been written in 1914, since Jones stayed in Budapest during June and July 1913. He saw Ferenczi for two hours of training analysis every day (see *Freud–Ferenczi, 1*, pp. 489–501 and *Freud–Jones*, pp. 200–214). Concerning Ferenczi's planned visit to England, see also Ferenczi's letter to Freud on 20 July 1914 (*Freud–Ferenczi, 2*, pp. 5–6), and Jones' letter to Freud on 27 July 1914 (*Freud–Jones*, pp. 295–296).
2. The outbreak of the First World War prevented Ferenczi from going.
3. See Abraham's circular dated 10 March 1914 in *Die Rundbriefe, 1*, pp. 35–36.

15F

Visegrád, 26 July 1914

Mr. Prof. Dr. Ernest Jones
69 Portland Court
London W.[1]

Most cordial regards from the old Visegrad Clan.

Dr. Schächter[2]

Thane of the Clan, Ferenczi, and Dr. Bakody about to join the army![3]

Bakody Aurélné
Mrs Bakody
Anti Schächter

Gabor Schächter
Franz Schächter

Warm regards from Puzi,[4] Jozefin, Zichy,[5] Klári

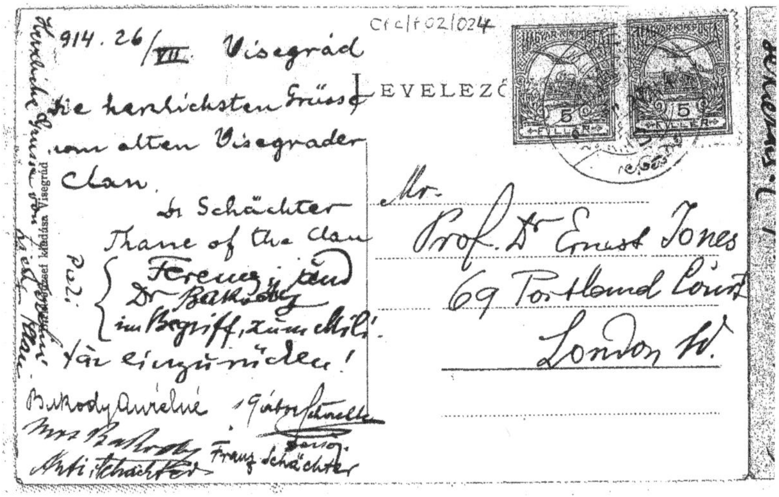
914. 26/VII. Visegrád

Die herzlichsten Grüsse vom alten Visegrader Clan.

Dr Schächter
Thane of the Clan

Ferenczi und Dr Bakody

Bakody Aurélné

Mrs Bakody

Franz Schächter

LEVELEZŐ

Mr.
Prof. Dr Ernest Jones
69 Portland Court
London W.

Postcard from Dr. Schächter and others to Jones.

Notes to letter 15F

1. Picture postcard.
2. In Dr. Schächter's handwriting. Miksa Schächter (1859–1917), was a physician and paternal friend of Ferenczi. Editor-in-chief of the journal *Gyógyászat* (The Art of Healing), which published many of Ferenczi's papers. See Ferenczi's obituary, "My friendship with Max Schächter", in *Gyógyászat*, 30 December 1917 (Ferenczi, 1917[199]).
3. In Ferenczi's handwriting.
4. Difficult to decipher.
5. Difficult to decipher.

16F

[Budapest] 29/7 1914
(London 31/7)[1]

Dear Friend!

Unfortunately it has become a certainty that I will not be allowed to leave the country. The nice time I had hoped to spend in London I shall have to spend here now and—wait to be called up. It is quite possible I will have to report for military duty and join in the campaign as a physician, on horseback with the Hussars!![2]

I will not write to you about the conditions here; you are, of course, familiar with them from the newspapers. England is looked upon with much sympathy here, in contrast to the other two "entente" powers.

Kind regards!
Ferenczi

Maeder[3] announced his resignation from the Association to me today. They are founding a new, independent psychological organisation.[4]

Notes to letter 16F

1. The date—probably the date of the postmark—as well as the date between brackets are in an unknown hand.
2. Ferenczi joined the 7th Honvéd Hussar-Regiment in Pápa on 24 October 1914 as Chief Medical Officer in the Hungarian Hussars.
3. Corrected in the original from "Jung".
4. The Zurich Association of psychoanalysts seceded from the International Psychoanalytical Association on 10 July 1914 and reformed as the Association for Analytical Psychology four months later.

17F

Pápa,[1] 15 May 1915

Dear Friend,

My warmest thanks to you for actually managing to complete the arduous and boring task of translating my works,[2] news of which reached me via Rank. I appreciate the pains you have taken as an expression of your friendship and feel sure that this affection is strong enough even to outlast the long isolation.

I have nothing special to report about myself. Since the end of Oct[ober], I have been doing military service in a Hussar regiment, although only behind the lines for now, where there is little to do. I even see 2–3 private patients for analysis every day. Apart from that, I am thinking about problems on the frontier of psychology and biology; whether something useful will come of it is very much in doubt. Physically, I am very well, helped by the provincial calm and my daily rides.

You will be interested to know that a Prof. Levy-Bianchini from Salerno[3] wants to translate my paper on "Introjection" into Italian.[4] Strange contrast between this Internationalisation and the current battles among nations!

Warm regards!
Write if possible.

Ferenczi

Kind regards and many thanks to Dr Emden.[5]

Barracks of the Hussar regiment in Pápa.

Notes to letter 17F

1. Pápa is a small town about 125 km south-west of Budapest.
2. Ferenczi's (1916[186]) *Contributions to Psycho-Analysis,* containing fifteen papers translated from German by Ernest Jones, was published in 1916 by R. C. Badger in Boston and Stanley Phillips in London.
3. Marco Levi-Bianchini (1875–1961) was Professor of Psychiatry in Naples. In 1919, he met Edoardo Weiss and founded the first unofficial psychoanalytic group in Italy. From 1922–1936, he was a Member of the Vienna Psychoanalytic Association and became a founding member of the Italian Psychoanalytic Association in 1925, serving as its honorary President until his death. His plan to translate Ferenczi's paper came to nothing. He was already in correspondence with Freud about translating his "Five lectures on psycho-analysis" (1910a), published in 1915 as the inaugural volume of the series *Biblioteca Psichiatrica Internazionale,* which he founded (see *Freud–Ferenczi, 2,* pp. 21–23). He also edited *Il Manicomio* from 1913 and founded the *Archivio Generale di Neurologia e Psichiatria* in 1920.
4. "Introjektion und Übertragung" appeared in the *Jahrbuch* (Ferenczi, 1909[67]), and was translated as "Introjection and transference" by Jones (see Ferenczi, 1916[186], pp. 35–93).
5. Jan E. G. Van Emden (1868–1950), a physician, was one of the pioneers of psychoanalysis in Holland and a personal friend of the Freud family. In 1919, he became President of the Dutch Psychoanalytic Association. In the war period, Emden received and forwarded mail between Vienna and London. Ferenczi may be thanking him for doing the same with his mail to Jones.

18F

ca. 24 July 1916[1]

Dear Jones,

Many thanks for your kindness and your interesting letter. What a shame that you cannot come and see me for a few weeks at least. I would have taught you interesting psycho-technical things.

Do you know anything about the fate of my American[2] translation? I only ever see the announcements in the I[nternational] J[ournal of] Abnormal Psychology.

I believe that we will meet up again sooner than you think. I hear your first destination is Vienna. I want to be in the party!

The dream was most interesting. Strange, though, that here as there, there is talk of Sir.[3]

Kind regards,
Ferenczi

Notes to letter 18F

1. The date "ca 24/7/16" on the original is in an unknown hand. Ferenczi might have been writing from Mária Valéria barrack hospital in Budapest, where he was stationed.
2. Corrected in the original from "English". Ferenczi is referring to Jones' translation and editing of his papers in *Contributions* (1916). Jones had secured Badger as publisher in Boston who had an arrangement with Stanley Phillips in London to publish his books in England. Jones had reported to Freud on 30 May that the proofs had arrived (*Freud–Jones*, p. 318).
3. Difficult to decipher.

[18aF]

12 June 1921[1]

Frau Klein[2] ought to have informed us too about her resignation from the Budapest group and given more detailed reasons. With regard to this I consulted Dr. Rado by the way.

Notes to letter 18aF

1. The original of this letter is missing from the BPAS Archives. Phyllis Grosskurth quotes from this letter in her book on Melanie Klein, referring to the "Jones Archive" (Grosskurth, 1986, p. 94).
2. Melanie Klein became a member of the Hungarian Society in July 1919. She left Budapest shortly after her husband went to work in Sweden, and in 1921 she moved to Berlin where Karl Abraham, whom she had met at the Hague Congress (8–11 September 1920), was working. See King and Steiner, 1991, p. 18.

19F

International Zeitschrift
für ärztl. Psychoanalyse[1]
Herausgegeben von Professor
Dr. Sigm. Freud
Schriftleitung: Dr S. Ferenczi, Budapest,
VII. Elisabethring 54, Dr Otto Rank, Wien,
IX/4, Simondenkgasse 8.
Verlag Hugo Heller & Cie., Wien I.
Bauernmarkt 3.

Mr. Ernest Jones M.D.
London W1
Harley Street 111
B[uda]pest, 11.July 1921

Dear Friend,

Many thanks for letter and photos. Nothing to report from here save my address for the summer, f[rom] 2nd August: Tegernsee (Bavaria), Hotel Bayrischer Hof.[2] Will notify you of changes of address in good time.

Regards from ourselves to you all,

Ferenczi

Notes to letter 19F

1. Postcard with printed sender address, henceforth "Internationale Zeitschrift für ärztl. Pychoanalyse".
2. Ferenczi had written a similar note to Freud on the same day to which he had added a postscript: "the state of my health wobbly" (*Freud–Ferenczi, 3*, p. 59). Because of ill-health, Ferenczi went instead to the nearby health-spa, Dr Wigger's Kurheim, at Garmisch-Partenkirchen (see *Freud–Ferenczi, 3*, pp. 64–65). The following day, Ferenczi sent an almost identical postcard as a *Rundbrief* (*Die Rundbriefe, 2*, p. 220).

20F

Internationale Zeitschrift
für ärztl. Psychoanalyse
Dr. Ferenczi, Budapest, Nagydiófa u.3.[1]

Dr. Ernest Jones MRCP.
London WC1
Harley Street 111.

Budapest, 22.I.1922 [London, 26th Jan 1922]

Dear Friend,

From here, all there is to report is that your letter of 11/I[2] did not arrive.—I repeated the lecture on metapsychology[3] in the Association. One of our members announced popular lectures in a business club without checking this with the Association first. Members were advised accordingly.[4] Pierce Clark[5] sent me an appreciative letter about the tic paper,[6] expressing agreement. What can you tell me about Pierce Clark?[7]

Kind regards,

Ferenczi

Notes to letter 20F

1. Postcard with printed sender address, and Ferenczi's address in Budapest in handwriting.
2. Jones had written a *Rundbrief* on 11 January 1922 (*Die Rundbriefe, 3*, pp. 17–19).
3. At the invitation of English and American psychoanalysts, on 6 January 1922 Ferenczi gave his lecture on "The progress of individual psychology in Freud's 'Group Psychology and the Analysis of the Ego'" in Vienna. He presented the lecture again on 15 January 1922 in Budapest, and published in the *Zeitschrift*, (*8*[1922]: 206–209) under the title "Der individualpsychologische Fortschritt in Freuds 'Massenpsychology und Ich-Analyse'". He also published it in Hungarian on 18 June 1922 in *Gyógyászat*, (*62*[25]: 360–363) (see also Ferenczi, 1922[244]).
4. Most probably it is about Zsigmond (Sigmund) Pfeifer. On the same day, Ferenczi wrote in his *Rundbrief*, "Pfeifer now gives popular lecture on psychoanalysis in a business club, announced without asking the Association. I gave proper instructions to the members" (*Die Rundbriefe, 3*, p. 35).

   Pfeifer Zsigmond (Sigmund) (1889–1945), was a Hungarian neurologist and psychoanalyst. He obtained his medical degree in Budapest (1912), and was a member of the Galileo Circle. He became member of the Hungarian Psychoanalytic Association in 1918, on the basis of his psychoanalytic work on children's play (Pfeifer, 1919; see also *Freud–Ferenczi, 2*, pp. 162, 279). He was trained by Ferenczi and Vilma Kovács. He died in the Buchenwald concentration camp.
5. Pierce Clark (1870–1933) was a neurologist, specialising in epilepsy at Manhattan State Hospital. From 1913, he was a member of the New York Psychoanalytic Association. His lecture "Psychological studies on the nature and pathogenesis of epilepsy, with discussion" appeared in the *Zeitschrift 3*(1915): 175–179. He quit the New York Association in 1926, but remained a member of the American Association. For Ferenczi's own later opinion of Clark, see his letter to Freud dated 30 June 1927 (*Freud–Ferenczi, 3*, p. 312).
6. Ferenczi's "Psychoanalytische Betrachtungen über den Tic" ("Psychoanalytic considerations regarding the tic") appeared in the *Zeitschrift*, *7*(1921): 33–62 (Ferenczi, 1921[232]).
7. Jones answered Ferenczi's question in his *Rundbrief* of 31 January:

   > You ask about Pierce Clark. He is a good clinician and a pleasant man personally. He has done much useful work on epilepsy,

though Mc Curdy tells me he stole it from him. His attitude towards Psa. is ambivalent, partly owing to the difficulty of official people in N.Y. associating themselves with the rather unfortunate crowd who are connected with Psa, e.g. Jelliffe, Tannenbaum, etc. Also I believe he does not get on with Brill. (*Die Rundbriefe, 3,* pp. 36–37)

21F

Internationale Zeitschrift
für ärztl. Psychoanalyse[1]
Dr. Ferenczi, Budapest, Nagydiófa u.3.

Dr. Ernest Jones M.R.C.P.
London W.1
111. Harley Street

Budapest, 20.II.1922.

Dear Ernest,

In the matter of Dr. Bose,[2] I must entrust myself to your judgement entirely, since you know him and the way in which he manages things in Calcutta best. Though it might be prudent for the time being—at least until the Berlin Congress—to only agree a provisional affiliation to the British group and to postpone the conferment of independent group status until the group has proven its abilities.[3] In any case, it would be good if we could get to know the Indian psychoanalysts in Berlin.

Kind regards from my wife too, to yourself and Mrs. Jones,[4]

Ferenczi

Notes to letter 21F

1. Postcard with printed sender address.
2. Girindrasekhar Bose (1887–1953) was a psychologist and an early supporter of psychoanalysis in India. He lectured on psychoanalysis at Calcutta university from 1917 and founded the Indian Psycho-Analytical Society on 22 January 1922. His efforts were recognised with becoming co-editor of the *Zeitschrift* and the *International Journal of Psycho-Analysis* in 1923. Jones' judgement of Bose is clear from his letter to Freud dated 13 February 1922:

   > Dr. Bose has constituted an Indian Psychoanalytical Society and has formally applied for affiliation into the International. He has sent a complete list of their statutes which are modelled on the British ones. Everything is conducted in a most orderly way, and I myself am satisfied to accept them. (*Freud–Jones*, p. 460)

3. In his *Rundbrief* of 2 March 1922, Jones reported "I have personally accepted the Indian Group and begged Bose to come to the Congress. Ferenczi's suggestion (made privately) that we should temporarily attach them to the London group I do not find very practical" (*Die Rundbriefe, 3*, p. 76). The provisional acceptance of the Indian Psycho-Analytical Society in March 1922 was ratified by the Berlin Congress. Ferenczi might have been suggesting a provisional affiliation to the British Society because several members of the Indian Society, including Bose, were already members of the British Society in 1922. When the Indian Society became a component society of the International Psychoanalytical Association, they transferred their membership.
4. Katharina (Kitty) Jokl (1892–1983), was the second wife of Jones. He first met her in Zurich in September 1919, on his way to Vienna, having corresponded with her from May after he had tried to hire her as his secretary at the suggestion of Hanns Sachs. The couple married on 9 October in Zurich. Katharina came from a non-observant Jewish family, and had a degree in economics (see Maddox, 2006, pp. 151–156).

22F

Dr. Ernest Jones
London W.1.
Harley Street 81.[1]

[Budapest] 22nd Oct[ober] [19]22.

D[ear] Fr[iend]!

This time just a substitute *Rundbrief* [circular]. Detailed report to follow on 1st November.

First meeting 8 days ago; topic: report on Congress.[2] Generally much appreciation for C[ongress] organisation and Berlin hospitality. Local newspapers and a med[ical] journal reproduced the programme.

During Radó's absence,[3] Mrs Radó-Révész[4] is deputising for the secretary. (Bp. IX. Ferencz Körút 14.)

Poor Pfeifer's[5] apartment was completely cleaned out while he was in Berlin.[6]

Cordially,

Sándor Ferenczi

Private matters: my wife says thank you for the information and will obtain the requested facts.

Notes to letter 22F

1. Postcard.
2. The Seventh International Psychoanalytic Congress took place in Berlin from 25 to 27 September 1922. Jones was re-elected President, and Ferenczi spoke about his theory of genitality. For a report on the Congress, see the *Zeitschrift*, *8*(1922): 478–505 and *Bul. Int. Psychoanal. Assn.*, *4*(1923): 235–243.
3. Sándor Radó emigrated to Berlin in the autumn of 1922, where he was analysed by Karl Abraham. See Roazen and Swerdloff, 1995, pp. 179–181.
4. Erzsébet Révész (1887–1923), was a neurologist and a member first of the Vienna, then of the Hungarian, Psychoanalytic Association. She married Sándor Radó in 1919. Analysed by Freud, she died while engaged in a second analysis with Ferenczi.
5. Zsigmond (Sigmund) Pfeifer, see letter 20F, note 4.
6. At the Berlin congress, Pfeifer lectured on "Musikpsychologische Probleme" (Problems of the psychology of music] (*Zeitschrift*, *8*[1922]: 498).

23F

INTERNATIONALE ZEITSCHRIFT FÜR
ÄRZTLICHE PSYCHOANALYSE

B[uda]p[est], 6th July 1923

Dear Ernest. (Instead of a *Rundbrief*!)

Having thought it over a great deal, I decided to forego the trip to England.[1]—Much as it grieves me to miss this long-awaited opportunity to visit England and to see you again.

There is nothing much to say regarding scientific and political matters here. A candidate by the name of Mrs. Kovács,[2] translator of "Beyond the Pleasure Principle", a wealthy lady, is making the case for a psychoanalytic clinic to me; she currently treats 5 pat[ients] (amongst them two doctors in training) almost for free.

Not long ago, I finally sent Mrs Herford[3] home. I must say, she has made very good progress. I even succeeded, so I believe, in reducing her seemingly incurable anagogy. As far as I am concerned, she would make a useful member of your group. I should be interested to hear your views on this.

On 16/17. my wife and I will travel to Klobenstein am Ritten (near Bozen,[4] Italy), where the Ranks will be too.[5] I am happy to meet in Wolkenstein.[6] My wife probably will not come.

Please be so kind as to ask[7] the organisers of the Oxf[ord] Congress, whether I have to pay the membership dues, even although I will not be able to attend (I will write directly as well). It is not a trivial sum by our standards. Again many thanks for the eagerness, with which you encouraged my trip to England and were prepared to receive me.

My wife and I send best wishes to you both,
Sándor

Vilma Kovács (1883–1940).

Notes to Letter 23F

1. Ferenczi had planned to attend the International Congress of Psychology in Oxford, to be held from 27 July to 1 August 1923. In a letter to Freud on 15 July 1923, Ferenczi told him: "I have given up the trip to Oxford, which would have greatly fragmented my vacation" (*Freud–Ferenczi, 3,* p. 109). Ferenczi was occupied with writing *Thalassa* (*Freud–Ferenczi, 3,* p. 110), and probably wanted uninterrupted time to pursue his work.
2. Vilma Kovács, née Prosznitz (1883–1940), was the central "mother figure" of the Hungarian Psychoanalytic Association. At the age of fifteen, she had married the cousin of her sister's husband Zsigmond Székely, twenty-two years her senior. One of her daughters, Alice Székely-Kovács, also became a psychoanalyst and Michael Bálint's first wife. Her other daughter, Olga Székely-Kovács, was an artist whose own daughter, Judith Dupont, is a psychoanalyst in France and the literary executor and publisher of several of Ferenczi's works. Vilma Kovács later married the architect Frigyes Kovács, with whom she supported Hungarian psychoanalysis, setting up a psychoanalytic clinic in 1931. Prompted by her agoraphobia, Vilma consulted with Ferenczi around 1921. He took her into analysis and became her training analyst. She became a member of the Hungarian Psychoanalytic Association in 1924 and chair of its Training Committee in 1925. Her paper "Lehranalyse und Kontrollanalyse" (Kovács, 1933) ("Training and control analysis", Kovács, 1936) remains a classic text. In 1923, she translated into Hungarian Freud's *Beyond the Pleasure Principle* (*A halálösztön és az életösztönök.* Budapest: Világirodalom).
3. Ethilda Budgett-Meakin Herford (1872–1956), a physician, became an associate member of the British Psycho-Analytical Society in 1921 and a member in 1934. She first had analysis with J. C. Flügel (see *Die Rundbrief,* 1, p. 172), then with Abraham, and entered training analysis with Ferenczi in 1922. (See *Freud–Ferenczi, 3,* pp. 106–107.) Her suitability for analytic training was often hotly debated within the Committee: Jones, in particular, disapproved of her. She translated three of Freud's works into English.
4. Above this, Ferenczi wrote "Hotel Post".
5. Ferenczi and his wife travelled to Klobenstein on 16 July 1923, where they met not only the Ranks, but also Mathilde Freud and Robert Hollitscher. Ferenczi describes this stay in Klobenstein in a letter to Freud dated 25 July 1923 (*Freud–Ferenczi, 3,* p. 110). Ferenczi and Rank consulted over their "would-be prize work" *Entwicklungsziele der Psychoanalyse,* published the following year (Ferenczi & Rank, 1924).

6. The Committee planned to meet at Wolkenstein (Selva di Val Gardena) in August (*Freud–Ferenczi, 3*, p. 108). In the event, they "met at Castell Toblino on 26 August and went on to stay at San Cristoforo" (*Jones, 3*, p. 98).
7. Over "to ask whether", Ferenczi wrote "to tell that".

24F

Budapest, 7th[1] Oct[ober] 1923

Dear Ernest,

I thank you most warmly for your news and am very sorry to hear that once again you are having trouble with your health.[2] I hope you will now be free of this kind of worry for a long time.

You are, no doubt, already aware of the Prof[essor]'s condition. On his return, the new growth was found to be progressing decidedly too fast, so that Hayek[3] proposed radical surgery (having explained the facts of the case to the Prof. first). The Prof. agreed without further ado, became much calmer, in fact, and productive again for the first time in quite a while. I was able to convince myself of this personally, since I spent last Sunday in Vienna. The operation will be performed in two stages: first (a few, small) glands will be removed, and a day later the diseased bone itself; it will be carried out by the renowned oral surgeon Dr. Pichler.[4] The Prof. will stay at the Auersperg Sanatorium (most likely, he is there already, but I have not heard yet.[5])

With regards to your personal question, I can only reiterate what I already told you more than once in S[an] Cristoforo:[6] I do not consider you an out-and-out neurotic either, but am firmly of the opinion that you are in need of analysis, not only because of your, as I believe, unconsciously motivated actions, but also because I must consider your previous analysis incomplete just on the grounds of my technique having been far less perfected at the time. I thus think further analysis desirable, if for no other reason than the sake of your own analytic practice. However, if we were to start a proper analysis this time, we should not (although my analyses are much shorter these days) allow it to be constrained by any predetermination of length or termination date. How this might fit with the demands of your life I am, of course, unable to judge.

N.B: as far as the letter to Brill is concerned, the exact wording is much less important than the general feeling it gave expression to.

Here, things are quiet,—I have more than[7] enough work,—but altogether still too little for these expensive times.

With kind regards to yourself and your loved ones,

Sándor

I should be delighted to receive some personal news from you too now and again.

Notes to letter 24F

1. Corrected from "6th".
2. On 12 September 1923, Jones wrote to Freud:

   > I had counted on sending you a letter in Rome – but all intentions bow before physical conditions. I have had 12 days of the most severe influenza imaginable (temp. 40°C for three days, pleurisy, intestinal complications, etc.), and am still very weak. (*Freud–Jones*, p. 256)

3. Marcus Hajek (1861–1941) was Professor of Laryngology at Vienna University. According to Schur, although Hajek had conducted valuable research on the anatomy of the sinuses "he was generally known to be a somewhat mediocre surgeon. . . ." (Schur, 1972, p. 351). Hajek made the first, botched operation on Freud's jaw on 20 April 1923.
4. Hans Pichler (1877–1949), head of a newly established ward specialising in oral surgery at the Vienna surgical hospital, became Freud's surgeon. The operation, during which the entire upper jaw and palate on the affected side were removed, took place on the 4th and 11th October 1923.
5. "Yet" inserted later.
6. On 26 August 1923, the Committee met in San Cristoforo, near Freud's summer residence (Lavarone), albeit without Freud, who received the group on 29 August. The chief topic of the San Cristoforo meeting—besides Freud's cancer—was the extraordinarily sharp disagreement between Rank and Jones. Ferenczi had foreseen a difficult meeting when he wrote to Freud on 21 August of the difficulties with Jones, all the "more difficult, since personal factors also figure in them. But we think it is not yet time to act more energetically against him, although we want to call him to account for certain things" (*Freud–Ferenczi, 3*. p. 112). On 26 August 1923, Jones wrote to his wife Katharine,

   > We have spent the whole day thrashing out the Rank–Jones affair. Very painful but I hope our relations will now be better and believe so, but on the other hand expect Ferenczi will hardly speak to me for Brill has just been there and told him I had said Rank was a swindling Jew (stark übertrieben [grossly exaggerated]). Brill of course has gone back to U.S.A. without seeing me. (BPAS Archives)

   On 28 August 1923, he added,

> The whole community, after hours of talking and shouting . . . decided that I was in the wrong in the Rank–Jones affaire, in fact that I am neurotic. A Jewish family council sitting on one sinner must be a great affair, but picture it when the whole five are insisting on analysing him on the spot and altogether! (BPAS Archives)

Rank even demanded that Jones be excluded from the Committee but, at Abraham's insistence, this did not happen.

7. "More than" was inserted later.

25F

Budapest, 13.I.[19]24.

Dear Ernest,

I am adding a few lines of a private nature to the *Rundbrief*.[1] This post hoc examination of the motives on either side, which have led to this disagreement between us, is difficult to conduct satisfactorily from a distance. I could, in fact, raise quite a few[2] objections to the argument you have mounted, but feel it is time to put the matter to rest. Still, I cannot refrain from pointing out that a complete stranger (I cannot even recall his name) would hardly write about the topic you deal with and not use my theory as a starting point. I do not believe that this affair[3] will mar our relationship forever, or even in the short term, and hope the future will offer us both opportunities to demonstrate good will and kindness.

In hope, I remain yours with best wishes,

Sándor

Notes to letter 25F

1. Ferenczi wrote a *Rundbrief* the same day (*Die Rundbriefe*, *4*, pp. 151–152).
2. Ferenczi crossed out his original "a lot of" and replaced it with "a few".
3. The publication of Jones' "The nature of auto-suggestion" (Jones, 1923a) opened up an old wound for Ferenczi. More than a decade earlier, he had accused Jones of plagiarism. According to Ferenczi, Jones plagiarised his theory of suggestion set out in "Introjection and transference" (Ferenczi, 1909[67]) in his paper on "The action of suggestion in psychotherapy" (Jones, 1911). Ferenczi now felt Jones had repeated the offence and he remonstrated with him. In his *Rundbrief* of 2 November 1923, Ferenczi had once again accused Jones of plagiarism (*Die Rundbriefe*, *4*, p. 121) and Jones had responded in detail in his *Rundbrief* of 12 November (*Die Rundbriefe*, *4*, pp. 127–130). The two men could not agree. Jones wrote on 15 December of Ferenczi being "unable to accept my apology and explanation" and proposed a solution put forward by Abraham of publishing a letter in the *British Journal of Medical Psychology*, edited by T. W. Mitchell. Jones sent a draft letter to Ferenczi, but it was neither circulated to the Committee for comment as planned nor did it appear in print (*Die Rundbriefe*, *4*, pp. 144, 153). On 20 December1923, Ferenczi wrote to Freud of his "energetic coming out against Jones" (*Freud–Ferenczi*, *3*, pp. 116–117, and see also Ferenczi's *Rundbrief* dated 2 December 1923, *Die Rundbriefe*, *4*, pp. 137–139).

26F

B[uda]pest, 10.IV.1924.

Dear Ernest,

My thanks for sending me your manuscript,[1] as well as your kind words on the occasion of my "Gen[ital] Th[eory]"[2] appearing in print.—It is, of course, not possible to discuss your objections by letter;[3] I hope we will have the opportunity in Salzburg.[4]

I also have yet to thank you for the wonderful book (Applied Ps[ycho] A[nalysis][5]).

Hope to see you soon and regards to Mrs Jones also,

Sándor

Notes to letter 26F

1. It is not altogether clear which manuscript this refers to, but it might have been "Psycho-analysis and anthropology", which Jones had read to the Royal Anthropological Society on 19 February (Jones, 1924a).
2. *Versuch einer Genitaltheorie* (*Thalassa; Theory of Genitality*) (Ferenczi, 1924[268]).
3. See Jones's *Rundbrief* on 18.2.1924, concerning *Entwicklungsziele der Psychoanalyse*: "But this general question of co-operation is one that cannot be well discussed in a letter" (*Die Rundbriefe, 4*, p. 176).
4. Ferenczi is referring to the Eighth International Psychoanalytic Congress in Salzburg from 21 to 23 April 1924, which Freud did not attend. During the Congress, Abraham was elected President and Eitingon Secretary of the International Psychoanalytical Association. For a report on the Congress, see Abraham's report in the *Zeitschrift, 10*(1924): 211–218 and Abraham and Jones's in *Bul. Int. Psychoanal. Assn., 5*(1924): 391–408.
5. *Essays in Applied Psychoanalysis*, London: International Psychoanalytic Press (Jones, 1923b).

27F

Budapest, 6th July 1924

Dear Ernest,

Having just had some time to read the latest volume of your "Journal", I am taking this opportunity to thank you for kindly sending it to me.

The time spent in Budapest by the English colleagues (from whom, incidentally, I have not heard since their departure) was a kind of English–Hungarian avowal of psychoanalytic friendship, which, by the way, only seems a continuation of the old sympathy between our countries.[1]

You will probably be most interested in what I can say about the condition of the Professor. Fortunately, there is only good news. There is no sign of a recurrence objectively, which is all the more significant because almost three quarters of a year have gone by already since the operation. Subjectively, he is up and down, not too bad altogether. It is to be hoped that the summer vacation will bring a decided increase in strength.

Myself, I was working flat out until 1st July, have been only three quarters full since, and am living in a garden near the city. Hot, but more bearable. In August, I will probably go to the mountains (Italian Tyrol).[2] An invitation to travel to America has come to nothing.[3]

Best regards from my wife and me to both of you,

Sándor Ferenczi

Notes to letter 27F

1. The Glovers and three British analysts had accompanied Róheim to Budapest on 26 April after the Salzburg Congress where James Glover had given a paper. Ferenczi "inaugurated an English Society meeting in their honour" over which he presided in English and at which Róheim spoke in English on "Dreams and adaptation in the history of mankind", a paper "strongly influenced by the genital theory and the birth trauma". Edward Glover's wife-to-be, Gladys, accompanied them. (See *Zeitschrift, 10*[1924]: 351; *Freud–Ferenczi, 3*, pp. 144–146. See also Ferenczi's letter to Otto Rank, in: *The Letters of Sigmund Freud & Otto Rank: Inside Psychoanalysis* (Lieberman & Kramer, 2012, pp. 203–204).)
2. In his letter to Freud on 30 June, Ferenczi wrote, "On July 1 we are moving into a boardinghouse near the city. Address: Dr. S. F., Budapest I., Rath Georg-Str. No. 5, Sanatorium 'Siesta.'" (*Freud–Ferenczi, 3*, p. 156). On 3 August, he wrote, "My wife and I are going to Engelberg (in Switzerland) on Friday. Address there: Hotel Edelweiss" (*Freud–Ferenczi, 3*, p. 158).
3. Rank had written enthusiastically to Ferenczi asking him to join him in America, but later became uncertain about the invitation and Ferenczi cancelled his travel plans (*Freud–Ferenczi, 3*, pp. 154–156).

28J

7th August 1924.[1]

Dear Sandor,

I was very pleased indeed to hear from you and to think that it betokens the continuance of good relations between us.[2] I cannot think of anything that would disturb this on the personal side. Even the slight scientific differences will, I hope, not become important, because I cannot identify you with Otto in this respect. I really fear he is repeating the history of Jung, and for the same neurotic reasons. No one identifies you with him in this respect, though it is a great puzzle to know how you came to write a book in common.[3]

I am working hard and shall have only two weeks' holiday. We have undertaken to complete the translation of the five volumes of the "Sammlungen" by an early date and this means intense pressure.[4] I hope you will enjoy your holiday in a more attractive place than New York, though no doubt you would find it interesting to renew your acquaintance with America and will probably do so in the course of time.

I have heard from various sources, including the best of all, excellent reports of Professor's health. His spirits also seem to have improved during his holiday and I even hear that he is writing various works.

I owe you for a long time an answer to your letter of last October in which you kindly offered to continue my analysis.[5] You will have guessed that the reason for the delay was that various matters, such as our unhappy suggestion controversy and the subsequent events connected with the Congress, made it inexpedient to enter into such personal matters, whereas now I feel freer to do so. I had, and still have, a strong desire to continue the analysis, chiefly because the most perfect attainable is the ideal we should all aim at in connection with psycho-analysis. On the other hand, the continuing expenses of my life and arrangements here make it absolutely impossible to be away from my work for more than the shortest time, which would obviously not be satisfactory. I can only console myself with the thought that anyone who is so happy in his love-life as I am and able to work so satisfactorily cannot be in any urgent need of further analysis, and I am sure you would agree with this criterion.

Sachs in London for two months[6] and Lampl[7] was also here for a few days. It has been very enjoyable seeing them.

With my kindest regards to yourself and your wife,

Yours always affectionately,[8]

Notes to letter 28J

1. The original is typewritten.
2. Jones wrote to Freud on 29 September 1924,

> Ferenczi and I have twice exchanged letters in the vacation, and I shall certainly continue as close contact as possible. I am very fond of him and know him well. I do not trace any suspicion of anti-analytic tendency in his work, but cannot refrain from the diagnosis of narcissism combined with poor judgement. (*Freud–Jones*, p. 555)

3. *Entwicklungsziele der Psychoanalyse* (Ferenczi & Rank, 1924).
4. Jones is referring to the five-volume *Sigmund Freud, M.D., LL.D. Collected Papers*, London: Hogarth Press, 1924–1925. On the significance of this translation for Jones, see Riccardo Steiner: "To explain our point of view to English readers in English words" (Steiner, 1991).
5. Ferenczi's letter was in fact dated 7 October 1923.
6. Sachs, who had analysed several London analysts, visited in August and September. In September he delivered a course of lectures before an invited audience of twenty-five people. The course occupied six evenings, the subject being "The technique of psycho-analysis" (see *Bul. Int. Psychoanal. Assn.*, 6[1925]: 101–102). Jones wrote to Freud on 12 August 1924,

> I have seen a good deal of Sachs since he has been in London. He has changed a good deal and is much more *schwerfällig* [sluggish]. I hope he will not incline towards melancholy as he grows older. I fear he is working too hard for his temperament. (*Freud–Jones*, p. 551)

7. Hans Lampl (1889–1958), a class-mate and friend of Martin Freud, studied medicine and practised for almost a decade before turning to psychoanalysis around 1921, when he moved to Berlin for a training analysis with Hanns Sachs. The following year he became an assistant at the "Berliner Poliklinik", where he met and married in 1925 Jeanne de Groot, who had been analysed by Freud. The couple returned to Vienna in 1933, becoming members of the Vienna Psychoanalytical Society. In 1938, they emigrated to Holland and joined the Dutch Society, remaining in Holland throughout the war period and beyond.
8. Signature missing.

29F

Engelberg, Hotel Edelweiß
18th Aug[ust] 1924.

Dear Ernest,

It has been a pleasure to hear from you again after quite some time. However, your letter or, rather, some sentences in your letter do require correction. You are absolutely right to say you must not identify me with Rank completely, when it comes to scientific matters; such complete identity is rare in science, especially where new ideas, like the ones Rank develops in his book on birth trauma,[1] are concerned. My "Genital Theory" would deal with the moment of birth somewhat differently; it also does not discuss the vicissitudes of this moment in the neuroses. And it is exactly this point over which I do not (or not yet) agree wholly with Rank's position, even although I am convinced he has added a great deal to what we know. It will be the task of further examination and research to bring Rank's idea into harmony with the main body of ps[ycho]a[nalytic] knowledge. As with all new things, there may be "exaggeration" in Rank's idea; it is, in any case, worthy of further thought.[2]

There may also be flaws in our joint book[3] (as I see it, flaws more of style and editing). Overall, I do, however, stand by the views expressed there; of course, such a very brief sketch is in need of manifold additions, corrections too perhaps, and I am not closing my mind to those.

I can understand the reasons which make it impossible for you to continue your analysis; it is well nigh impossible to abandon career and family for so long. Here I am thinking also[4] of the beautiful children's faces, a photograph of which I saw in Salzburg.[5] Please do send my regards, and those of my wife too, to the happy mother.

We arrived in Engelberg at the beginning of August (10th),[6] plan to stay here until Sept[ember] and then spend another couple of weeks, to 15th Sept[ember], elsewhere in Switzerland.

So far, we have been burning up and freezing by turns. But we enjoy the peace.

Again, kind regards,

Sándor

Notes to letter 29F

1. *Das Trauma der Geburt und seine Bedeutung für die Psychoanalyse* (Rank, 1924). English edition: *The Trauma of Birth and its Importance for Psychoanalysis* (Rank, 1929).
2. Ferenczi's judgement is echoed in the review of Rank's book by another member of the Committee, Hanns Sachs. In his comprehensive critique he concludes,

   > in spite of the one-sidedness and exaggeration which . . . characterize the book, psycho-analysis receives a valuable contribution in having attention drawn to the significance of the experience of birth, hitherto overlooked or underestimated, and that this may be reckoned as one more proof of Rank's psychological acumen. But progress along this line will certainly not take place . . . by one bold leap . . . but by patiently continuing to build on the firm and reliable foundations of psycho-analytical science. (Sachs, 1925, p. 508)

   Ferenczi later expressed severe reservations about the clinical development of Rank's birth trauma theory, concluding "we must regard Rank's technical experiment as a failure" (Ferenczi, 1927[277], p. 100).
3. *Entwicklungsziele der Psychoanalyse* (Ferenczi & Rank, 1924). Ferenczi was already aware of criticism of this work. In his review, which appeared the following year, Franz Alexander judged that "perfectly valid and often masterly descriptions of the analytic process are spoilt by the most untenable formulations" (Alexander, 1925, p. 495). Noting the American publication in the *International Journal* the following year, Jones simply referred readers to Alexander's review (Jones, 1926).
4. "Also" inserted later.
5. By this point the Joneses had two children, Gwenith and Mervyn, born in 1920 and 1922.
6. The Ferenczis found Engelberg too cold for comfort—"we almost froze to death," Ferenczi wrote to Freud. They moved on to the Hotel Eden at Montreux, by the end of the month. Ferenczi wrote to Freud of his plans: "We are staying here until about September 13, then we want to travel by way of Bern or Basel, [to] Germany, finally to Vienna at the end of September. I begin work in Budapest on October 1". Throughout the holiday in Switzerland Ferenczi gave three analytic hours, one to Eugenia Sokolnicka and two "to an English [female] colleague" (probably Ethilda Budgett-Meakin Herford) (*Freud–Ferenczi*, 3, pp. 162–163, 172).

30F

Budapest, 12th Oct[ober]1924

Dear Ernest,

Many thanks for your letter of 4th Oct[ober]. My practice is indeed full again and I have also been able to supply young colleagues with work and income. The material conditions are, however, quite precarious here.

Otto is, or is said to be, back from America[1] already; he is staying with his family in Merano, but has not got in touch as yet. I wrote to Reik[2] regarding the Wittels book;[3] unless it has already been given to someone else, you should review the book for both journals.[4]

I consider such joint reviews appropriate; Reik has responsibility for reviews[5] and I want to draw you to his attention.

On my return journey, I stopped off in Vienna and found the Professor in very good shape. He works 6 hours a day.[6]

Kind regards,

Sándor

Notes to letter 30F

1. Rank was in America from April to October 1924. He maintained a busy practice there and publicised his theoretical innovations. See "Dr. Rank in Amerika", *Zeitschrift, 10*(1924): 210.
2. Theodor Reik (1888–1969), psychologist, literary scholar, and philosopher, became a member of the Vienna Psychoanalytic Association in 1911. He wrote the first ever psychoanalytic doctoral thesis (*Die Psychogenese von Flauberts 'Versuchung des hl. Antonius'* (The psycho-genesis of Flaubert's 'Temptation of St. Anthony')). In 1913–1914 he had training analysis with Abraham in Berlin and, returning to Vienna, he became Secretary and Librarian of the Vienna Psychoanalytic Association in 1918. In 1928, he moved to Berlin, to The Hague in 1934, and finally, in 1938, he emigrated to New York. As a lay analyst, he was under threat of being banned from practising in the USA and founded his own "National Psychological Association for Psychoanalysis".
3. The reference is to Fritz Wittels' Freud biography *Sigmund Freud. Der Mann, die Lehre, die Schule* (Sigmund Freud. The man, the theory, the school of thought) (Wittels, 1924), which evolved out of a collaboration with Stekel.

   Fritz Wittels (1880–1950), a psychiatrist, was a member of the Wednesday Society from 1907. His relationship with Freud was complex. As early as 1908, he collaborated with Karl Kraus on his satirical review *Die Fackel*, which was critical of psychoanalysis. When he fell out acrimoniously with Kraus, Freud feared that the ill feeling between Wittels and Kraus might rebound on psychoanalysis and warned Wittels that his position in the Vienna Psychoanalytic Association was becoming "impossible" (see Timms, 1995, p. 95). He left the Association in 1910 and, after war service, joined Stekel, who analysed him. He returned to the Vienna Society in 1925 and was readmitted to membership around 1927. For Freud's reaction to Wittels' book, see his letter to Wittels dated 15 August 1924:

   > You know my attitude to this book; it has not become friendlier. I still maintain that someone who knows as little about a person as you do about me is not entitled to write a biography about that person. One waits till the person is dead, when he cannot do anything about it and fortunately no longer cares. (E. L. Freud, 1961, p. 350)

   In 1932 he amended his biography.
4. Jones' review of Wittels' book appeared in 1924 in both the *International*

Journal (5: 481–486) and the *Internationale Zeitschrift* (*10*: 342–347). Freud wrote to Jones on 23 October 1924 that Reik had sent him the proofs of Jones' reviews for the forthcoming *International Journal*, including the review of Wittels. Jones replied on 28 October, telling Freud that his review "was originally more severe, but Mrs. Riviere and my wife both thought it too much so, so I slightly softened it" (*Freud–Jones*, p. 558).

5. Reik oversaw reviews for the *Internationale Zeitschrift*.
6. In his letter dated September 21, 1924 in Baden-Baden, Ferenczi lets Freud know that he, on his way back, plans to visit him on September 27.

31F

Budapest, 29.V.1925

Dear Ernest,

I should have written to you a few days ago already, to support a plea from Róheim,[1] but have been prevented by various circumstances.—Róheim, whose predilection for all things Anglo-Saxon, particularly in his field of science, you will be familiar with, would like to give a lecture series or two on ps[ycho]an[alysis] and ethnology in London over the course of the summer (or, to be correct: in the autumn, after the Congress). He is thinking primarily of lectures for members of the ps[ycho]an[alytic] group, but of more public ones too, perhaps. He would like to earn enough from these to at least cover his (and his wife's[2]) expenses, during their stay in England. (He relies on this, since his—rather well-off, by the way—father is very stingy.) I should like to support his request and will add that he does <u>not</u> intend to use the opportunity to publicise those views, so unpopular with yourself, which he propounded in Salzburg; especially since he has, since, come to see his conclusions were exaggerated and is putting appropriate limits on his obsession with novelty.[3] As always, he will bring new and interesting ideas as well, but you should be able to convince yourself that he is changed in many respects and much[4] more open to discussion.—

Of your former patients, Major Daly[5] and Dr. Cole[6] are with me. The former continues to labour under his still not fully resolved castration-business, the latter on a relapse into (mostly neurotic) bronchial asthma.[7]—

How are you? How are your d[ear] wife and the children? I think it is time, now the scientific–political hatchet has been buried, we re-established our previously good personal relations. I am glad Róheim's request gave me an opportunity to write to you directly once again.

I am working a great deal, but just clinically. In terms of theory, nothing essential is going on with me; I think the way, in which the more <u>useful</u> innovations of last few years are finding their place in our present knowledge most interesting and am learning quite a bit, not just objectively, but about myself personally. I am inclined to call the current period one of "harmonisation"—surely more agreeable than the discord which occasionally reigned before.

Kind regards,

Sándor

I have heard nothing from Rank. I am hearing more and more about the technique he tried in America, though, which I now find to be wholly mistaken.[8] In <u>my</u> analyses, the "birth trauma" reduces itself to a neurotic phantasy.

Notes to letter 31F

1. Géza Róheim (1891–1953) was a Hungarian ethnologist and psychoanalyst, founder of ethno-psychoanalysis, who was in analysis with Ferenczi during 1915–1916 and later with Vilma Kovács. He went on to become the training analyst of Alice Bálint and István Székács-Schönberger, among others. Contrary to the widespread belief (see, for example, *Jones, 3*, pp. 12–13), Róheim was not appointed as university professor of anthropology in 1919. His application for university "Habilation" was rejected in 1917, and in 1919 he was only assigned to give popular lectures at the National Museum in Budapest. It should be noted that at that time there was no chair of anthropology at the University of Budapest (see Erős, 2011). In 1921, he won the Prize for Applied Psychoanalysis, the second year it was awarded, for "Das Selbst" (The self) (Róheim, 1921), and for his paper at the Sixth International Psycho-Analytic Congress at The Hague: "Central Australian Totemism" (abstracted in Abstracts of the Proceedings of the Sixth International Psycho-Analytical Congress, held at the Hague, 8 to 12 September, 1920. *Bul. Int. Psychoanal. Assn.*, *1*[1920]: 351–352. See also his book, *Australian Totemism. A Psychoanalytic Study in Anthropology* (Róheim, 1925)). From 1928 to 1931, he made expeditions to Somalia, Central Australia, Melanesia, and to the Yuma Indians in Arizona, all financed by Princess Marie Bonaparte on Freud's advice. He emigrated to America at the end of 1938, moving to New York in 1940, where he maintained an analytic practice. Ferenczi had asked Jones in September 1920 whether he could help to secure an academic post for Róheim in England, preferably in Cambridge. Jones sought assistance from W. H. Rivers, John Rickman, and David Eder, but in the end could not help (see *Rundbriefe, 1*, pp. 52, 71–72 and Rickman's letter to Róheim on 14 November (BPAS Archives)).
2. Parenthesis inserted later.
3. In a *Rundbrief* dated 26 November 1924, Abraham, Eitingon, and Sachs had sought Ferenczi's view on Rank's birth trauma, fearing that Róheim's paper at the Salzburg congress which drew on Rank's theory was influenced by Ferenczi (*Die Rundbriefe, 4*, pp. 198–199). Róheim's paper "Totemismus und Drachenkampf" (Totemism and dragon-fight) (*Zeitschrift, 10*(1924): 224–225) maintained that "Australian totemism revolves around the trauma of birth" and that "the dragon-fight is a repetition of the birth trauma, and the dragon a personification of the dangerous vagina" (*Freud–Abraham*, p. 523).
4. "Much" was inserted later.

5. Claud Dangar Daly (1884–1950), an Indian Army officer, had formerly been an analysand of Jones for a few months in 1916 and then Freud in 1920. In 1928, he became a member of the Indian Psycho-Analytical Society. Jones had not been impressed by Daly, and, for his part, Daly never forgave Jones for promising to complete his analysis after the war only to turn him away when the time came because he did not have space, sending him to Freud (see Robinson, 2002). In a letter to Freud dated 25 January 1920, referring to Daly, Jones advised Freud that "I analysed him for a few months four years ago. It is chiefly a question of foolish character traits, conceit and inferiority, slightly hysterical, rather an ass but easy to manage" *Freud–Jones*, p. 364). Freud was more generous, describing Daly in a letter to Ferenczi a couple of weeks after he had begun analysis with Ferenczi as "a simple person, but he sees correctly and is a good chap" (*Freud–Ferenczi, 3*, p. 212). Daly began analysis with Ferenczi on 1 April 1925 and continued for three and a half months before returning to India. He resumed analysis with Ferenczi in early 1926. In 1936, when he left the Indian army, he had further analysis with Freud. His dream diaries in the BPAS Archives show that he was indeed racked by anxieties about castration.
6. Estelle Maude Cole was a physician who became an associate member of the British Psychoanalytical Society, which she left in 1927. Already analysed by Jones, Freud turned her down for further analysis in 1922. She eventually found her way to Ferenczi, who, on 17 August 1922, wrote to Freud of her as "an English woman . . . who came here in order to learn 'active technique' from me, but instead of that had to experience a piece of normal analysis on her own person". Cole was his first English patient and to his "astonishment, it turned out that my English is, indeed, up to the task of moving forward with this patient" (*Freud–Ferenczi, 3*, p. 85). She returned to Ferenczi for further analysis in 1925.
7. According to Jones, Cole had almost died three years earlier "from pneumonia and heart failure" (*Die Rundbriefe, 3*, p. 93).
8. For Ferenczi's critique of Rank's technical innovations, see Ferenczi, 1927[277].

32J

5th June 1925[1]

Dear Sandor,

It was a great pleasure to hear from you directly and I wish to thank you for your kind and cordial letter. You may be sure that your sentiments are fully reciprocated. I am looking forward to seeing you in Homburg in September and hope that your wife will also be there.[2] We must talk over then the question of when you are coming to England. With the exception of Freud you are the only member of the Committee who has not visited us here and my wife and I often mention the matter to each other.

With regard to Róheim, I am altogether sympathetic to the idea and it is only a question of arrangement. I immediately telephoned to Rickman[3] and put the matter into his hands to work out the details. The thought struck us, however, that the date you suggest might not be the most favourable one. For instance, I could probably get the Royal Anthropological Institute to invite him to read a paper before them, but their programme for next Autumn is already made up. Then we should have preferred Róheim's course to be one of several that could be instituted to celebrate the opening of the clinic here, the date of which is unfortunately still uncertain. However, after going into the matter further with Rickman and others, I will write direct to Róheim and put the situation before him.[4] In the meantime, perhaps you would tell him that we welcome the idea and are doing our best to work it out.

A word or two about some of your analysands. Daly has some valuable qualities, intense energy being perhaps the highest. He is very deficient, however, in the matters of tact and makes himself rather unpopular and not adaptable to his social surroundings. His scientific writings are of considerable value, but are marred by complete inability to write grammatical English, which I dare say may be largely Komplexbedingt.[5] Dr. Cole we have spoken of before. From recent letters I see that she still retains much of her narcissistic overestimation. I am afraid her chances of securing much practice in London are very small, for the competition is very keen. Her decision whether to settle here or at some other place in England will, I suppose, depend partly on her private finances about which I know nothing. I saw recently Dr. Inman[6] who has applied for membership of the Society. He seems a clever fellow but decidedly unbalanced in his judgement, so we postponed his election. We should be glad of your opinion in the matter. Is he not somewhat hypomanic?

Life has been proceeding more quietly here since the stress of the Press business, 'Collected Papers', etc., is dying down. Psycho-analysis has,[7] I am sorry to say, made very little progress in England in the last year or two. Opposition to it, is very great and practice is not so good as it was. However, new students keep coming to re-inforce us and that I regard as the main thing. My family is a great source of joy to me and all its members are flourishing exceedingly well. The two Glovers[8] and I, with the three wives, are arranging to go to the Congress by motor, a four thousand kilometres' journey that makes a Rundreise[9] in France. It will last four or five weeks and should be very enjoyable.

With kindest regards,

Yours affectionately,[10]

Notes to letter 32J

1. The original is typewritten.
2. The Ninth International Psychoanalytic Congress took place in Bad Homburg from 3 to 5 September 1925. Initially, Lucerne or Geneva in Switzerland had been envisaged as congress venues. Bad Homburg was preferred for organisational reasons.
3. John Rickman (1891–1951), a British psychiatrist, began analysis with Freud in the Spring of 1920, continuing until 1922 when, on 4 October, he became a member of the British Psychoanalytical Society. Before long, he had established himself as a leading figure in British psychoanalysis, being particularly central in establishing the Institute in London and later serving as President of the British Society. From August 1928 through into late 1930, he was in analysis with Ferenczi, and later, from the mid-1930s until 1941, he turned to Melanie Klein for intermittent help (see King, 2003, p. 25). Rickman was Jones' most important collaborator in the *Press*, the short-lived British branch of the *Verlag*. As the Rickman–Róheim letters in the Archives of the British Psychoanalytical Society show, the two became good friends after Rickman's failed attempt to help Róheim find a post in England in 1920.
4. Jones wrote to Freud on 16 September 1925,

   > Róheim is in London at present giving us a course of lectures on some anthropological matters. He has apparently quite recovered from his temporary attack of *Geburtstrauma* [birth trauma] and is proving a welcome source of incitement to our members. He is also to read a paper before the Royal Anthropological Institute in a couple of weeks' time. (*Freud–Jones*, p. 581)

5. Complex dependent (German in the original).
6. Dr Samuel William Inman (1876–1968), consultant in eye surgery, came to psychoanalysis through his work in the Military Opthalmic Unit in Portsmouth where he worked with soldiers who were casualties of the First World War, alongside Millais Culpin, one of the pioneers of work with war-shock. He visited Freud in Vienna shortly after the war, who referred him to Ferenczi. In 1925, he joined the British Psychoanalytical Society. Inman pioneered the understanding of the emotional and psychological components of eye disorders.
7. Corrected from "is".
8. James Glover (1882–1926) and his younger brother Edward Glover (1888–1972) were both doctors and psychoanalysts. They had been in

analysis with Karl Abraham in Berlin at various times during the period 1920–1922. James Glover had directed the Medico-Psychological Clinic, Brunswick Square, before going on to play a key role in the British Psychoanalytical Society after his election as Associate Member (1921) and Member (1922). He died before he could take up the post of Assistant Director of the London Clinic of Psychoanalysis. Edward Glover, like his brother, was a key figure in the British Psychoanalytical Society following election to Associate Member and Member in the same years as his brother. With his brother's death, he took on the role of Assistant Director of the London Clinic and, in addition, held office as Scientific Secretary and as Director of Research. He resigned from the Society in 1944 in the aftermath of the Controversial Discussions (see the obituary of James Glover: Jones, 1927a; on Edward Glover see also Roazen, 2000).

9. Round trip (German in the original).
10. Signature missing.

33F

HOTEL ST. ANDREW
BROADWAY AT 72ND STREET
NEW YORK

Oct[ober] 5, 1926[1]

Dr. Ernest Jones,
81 Harley Street
London, W 1.

Dear Ernest:

Thank you for your letter and your Rundbrief.[2] This time I only write to inform you of my safe arrival in New York, and to say a few words about the Franklin case.[3] She has some peculiar character traits, and as you know I do regard character traits as a sort of private psychosis. Therefore your impression of her as "catatonic" is of course a bit exaggerated. She has great talent in analyzing neurotic as well as psychotic people. Please be a little more receptive to her, and you will find that she will reward your kindness with serious work that you can make use of in your new clinic.

Your Dr. Brill came to see me and we had a very good time together. He looks quite young and seems to be very contented. He has been invited to open the course of lectures which I begin today at the New School of Social Research.

With most heartfelt greetings to you and Mrs. Jones, I am,

Very cordially yours,

Sándor

Notes to letter 33F

1. The original is in English and typewritten except for the signature.
2. September 16, 1926 (*Die Rundbriefe, 4*, pp. 323–324).
3. Marjorie Ellen Franklin (1887–1975), a psychiatrist and member of the British Psychoanalytical Society, was in analysis with Ferenczi from 1924 until July 1926. In June 1926, Ferenczi sent her paper "Die bedingten Reflexe bei Epilepsie und der Wiederholungszwang" (Conditional reflexes in epilepsy and the repetition compulsion) to Freud for publication in the *Zeitschrift*. It finally appeared in *Imago* (Franklin, 1928). Ferenczi sketched a portrait of Franklin in a letter to Freud dated 4 July 1926:

> I couldn't very well talk Dr. Franklin out of visiting you. She is a somewhat peculiar person with very much knowledge and sharp logic. The analysis was able to ameliorate some of her character traits. She carried out three analyses under my direction. She is the niece of the former Viceroy of Palestine [Herbert Samuel] and the late English minister Montagu. Her father [is] a rich banker in London. She was in analysis for two and a half years. Naturally, you are <u>not</u> supposed to have learned all these data from me, that is to say, don't mention them in the event that she doesn't tell you about them herself. (*Freud–Ferenczi, 3*, p. 271)

Jones disliked Franklin and created difficulties in her being accepted into the British Psychoanalytical Society, despite Ferenczi's backing. When, later, Franklin wrote a letter of condolence to Ferenczi's widow, she replied that it had touched her profoundly because she recognised in it Ferenczi's own "heart-spirit" (BPAS Archives). Franklin went on to establish the Institute for the Scientific Study and Treatment of Delinquency (later the Portman Clinic) with fellow psychiatrists and psychoanalysts Edward Glover, Grace Pailthorpe, and Melitta Schmideberg.

34F

HOTEL ST. ANDREW
BROADWAY AT 72ND STREET
NEW YORK

December 13th, 1926[1]

Dear Ernest:

Your complaint against me in the case of Dr. Franklin is not justified. About two months ago I gave to her an official certificate but she was evidently too modest to take it to you; believing that, after being invited to work at the Institute, it was unnecessary.

Personally, I can only report that she really deserves the recommendation which I gave to you.[2] Of course, she still has some personal difficulties in her character but her capacities and scientific knowledge are so valuable that we must be lenient, all the more since she is constantly improving. And who of us is quite free from character difficulties? Of course, she needs the friendly support of her colleagues. Please influence them in this direction without divulging these rather personal details.

Thank you for your cooperation in the publishing of my "Contributions" [3] and accept for your whole family the best Christmas wishes from us both.

Yours cordially,

Sándor

Notes to letter 34F

1. The original was typewritten except for the signature and some corrections.
2. Ferenczi supplied her with a letter (23 October 1926, BPAS Archives) certifying that she had been in analysis with him for two and a half years and that she was now an analyst.
3. *Further Contributions to the Theory and Technique of Psychoanalysis.* London: Hogarth Press, 1926. The volume was compiled by John Rickman and translated by Jane Suttie and others.

35F

Baden-Baden, 26th June 1927
Werderstraße 14

Dear Ernest,

My wife and I will always remember the splendid reception afforded to us by yourself and Mrs Jones on the one hand, and by your Society on the other.[1] This time, I am only writing to assure you of this and to ask that you kindly use the next opportunity to also forward my most cordial thanks to the British group formally. I had the impression that the honour accorded me was not so much for my person, but for the Cause, whose oldest proponent I am. I should like to think too, however, that a good part of it was personal.—Thus, especially, the many tokens of exceptional kindness given to me by yourself and Mrs Jones.

Again, many thanks for everything—especially the wonderful day in Elstead!

We spent three pleasant days in Paris,[2] including an evening at Laforgue's[3] house. I share your view on this newest group leader's seriousness and reliability.

In Baden-Baden,[4] we were greeted by the news that my wife's purse had been handed in to the London police.[5] This brightens the only shadow over our memories of London. Please do let Mr. and Mrs. Fluegel[6] know too and convey our apologies for the somewhat low spirits with which we marred the nice lunch-party.

Kindest regards from ourselves to you all,

Sándor

Notes to letter 35F

1. The Ferenczis arrived at Southampton from America on 10 June. Ferenczi described his reception to Freud on 30 June:

> In Southampton we were received by Dr. Rickman, an interesting oddity. He drove us in his car across southern England to London, where we didn't arrive until the next evening. On the way he showed us churches, castles, typical English landscapes. We have become fond of England and London; it was my first visit to this country. Rickman was extraordinarily friendly with me.
>
> We spent twelve days in London; almost the entire time was devoted to invitations, lectures, conversations with individuals. Jones strove to heap every conceivable personal honor (in contrast to the American reception) upon me. (Meeting of the British group, with the request to lecture something to them; several large dinners, even a garden party in Jones's nice house.) Naturally, my former pupils Inman, Eder, Cole, used the occasion to testify to their friendship. The actual conversation with Jones took place in his country house [the Platt] in Elstead. I was mindful of your warning "Be careful". Actually, I found Jones's statements lacking in full and complete honesty. In lay analysis (the main topic of our conversation), he claims already to have found and shown the golden mean between the extremes (you and Brill); I also didn't succeed in moving him to admissions that to go beyond his suggestions that were published in the "Journal". It seems to me that that can sooner be effected by Eitingon; in this question I identify (as Jones says) too much with you, Herr Professor. (*Ferenczi–Freud, 3*, pp. 312–313)

Ferenczi addressed a Scientific Meeting of the BPAS on 15 June, reporting on his American trip. Two days earlier, he delivered his paper, "The adaptation of the family to the child: Being free-associations on children's education", to a joint meeting of the Medical and Educational Sections of the British Psychological Society (Ferenczi, 1928[281]).
Jones' version of the visit can be found in his letter to Freud dated 20 June 1927:

> Ferenczi's visit has been a great success here, though I am not so sure about the success of his American visit. It becomes clearer that his value lies essentially in the inspiration of his personality rather

> than in his intellectual judgements, for the latter are sometimes too strongly influenced by his phantasy. It was a very great pleasure having him here and I need hardly say the we are on the most excellent possible terms. (*Freud–Jones*, p. 620)

He also reported on the visit in his *Rundbrief* of 20 June 1927:

> During the ten days he has addressed two meetings and has spent every remaining minute in hospitable functions. He has made an extremely favourable impression everywhere and it had given us all great pleasure to have him amongst us in England. (*Die Rundbriefe*, *4*: p. 368)

2. Ferenczi described his time in Paris in a letter to Freud on 30 June 1927:

> We spent four days there, did some shopping, visited Sainte Chapelle, spent a Bohemian evening on Montmartre with new American friends . . . In Paris I got to know Laforgue somewhat better. He is a pleasant and reliable man, so it seems. The impression that Rank's birth theory made on him is softening. N.B. Rank is living like a king in Paris; he resides in a villa in the Bois de Boulogne, has a maître d'hotel and a chef de cuisine.—(Jones tells me he is doing good business in the stock market with the aid of American patients; otherwise, I also wouldn't be able to account for this degree of luxury.) Naturally, he also has a car and a chauffeur. To be sure, he has made himself look somewhat ridiculous by sending out his calling card with the telegram address "Ottoranks". That kind of thing is viewed as highly inappropriate in Paris.—The Princess was, unfortunately, not in Paris. (*Freud–Ferenczi*, *3*, pp. 313–314).

3. René Laforgue (1894–1962), a French psychiatrist and psychoanalyst was an analysand of Eugenia Sokolnicka (1923). He became a member of the Vienna Psychoanalytic Association in 1925 and in the following year co-founded and became the first President of the Societé Psychanalytique de Paris. Jones had reviewed favourably *La Psychanalyse et Les Névroses*, by Laforgue and Allendy (1924), see Jones, 1924b.
4. Ferenczi went on to Baden-Baden to stay with the Groddecks. In a letter to them from New York, he estimated he would arrive in Baden-Baden between 20 and 25 June (see *Ferenczi–Groddeck*, 2002, p. 79). He signed into the sanatorium guestbook on 26 June and signed out on 28 August (see *Ferenczi–Groddeck*, 2006, p. 140, note 5).

5. A fuller account of the incident can be found in Ferenczi's 30 June letter to Freud: "my wife left her purse with money and all her keys in a taxicab. . . . Here, in Baden-Baden, we then received the news from the London police that the purse had been turned in by the driver!" (*Freud–Ferenczi, 3*, p. 313).
6. John Carl Flügel (1884–1955), a British psychologist of partly German descent, was a social reformer, Professor of Psychology at University College, London (1929–1944), and psychoanalyst. He was Jones' trusted friend and ex-patient (see *Freud–Jones*, p. 342). A founder and lifelong member of the British Psychoanalytical Society, Flügel became Secretary of the IPA in 1919 until 1924, and Assistant Editor of the *International Journal of Psychoanalysis*. Beyond psychoanalysis, he played key roles in the British Psychological Society, becoming its President from 1932–1935.

36J

1st. February 1929.[1]

Dear Sándor,

I have been meaning to write to you for some time about Mrs. Rickman,[2] but both my wife and I have been ill for the past month and all activity has been reduced to a minimum. The point was this. Mrs. Rickman told me you had criticised me sharply for my attitude towards the question of her continuing her analysis, and this could only mean that she had misrepresented the situation to you or your attitude to me. Actually my views on the matter are very simple. From previous analytical experience of her I have good reasons to know her mentality and when this question was raised a couple of months ago I naturally probed at once into the question of motive. She made it quite plain that she had no inner need for analysis and that her only reason would be to please her husband, as on the former occasion. I naturally said then that there was no question of advising for or against such an analysis, because the idea was in the nature of things ruled out. No analysis could take place on that basis [!]. I am sure you would yourself have said the same thing in those circumstances.

The Council meeting in Paris which we arranged at the last Congress for Easter seems to have no luck. Both last year and this year I have made my plans on that basis and then begged for an arrangement four or five months beforehand. This time it has led to some correspondence with Anna, Eitingon[3] and van Ophuijsen and at the moment it does not seem likely that it will eventuate.[4] The only alternative seems to be a double meeting of Easterners and Westerners with Eitingon as a connecting link for both. It is a pity.

I am looking forward to a week or two's holiday in the South of France then to restore our health (my wife has just recovered from pneumonia). I hope that you both are in excellent health.

With all good wishes,

Yours always,[5]

Notes to letter 36J

1. The original is typewritten.
2. Lydia (Cooper Lewis) Rickman (1885–1971) was an American social worker from Chicago and wife of the psychoanalyst John Rickman (1891–1951). They met in Russia while working there for the Friends War Victims Relief Service, marrying in Russia in 1918. Lydia Rickman began her analysis with Jones in early October 1920 and continued into 1921 (*Freud–Jones*, pp. 391, 406, and see Pearl King's biography of Rickman (King, 2003, pp. 9–11).
3. Max Eitingon (1881–1943), born in Mogilev, Russia (today: Republic of Belarus), a physician and psychoanalyst, was an important patron of the psychoanalytic movement. Having studied medicine and philosophy in Marburg, he secured an internship at the Burghölzli in Zurich. He met Freud in 1907 and, in 1910, co-founded the Berlin Psychoanalytic Association, serving as its Secretary from 1922 and founding the Berlin Psychoanalytic Institute in 1920. In 1919, he joined the "Secret Committee", and from 1927–1932 was President of the International Psychoanalytic Association. He emigrated to Palestine in September 1933, and shortly afterwards founded the Palestine Psychoanalytic Society (Rolnik, 2012).
4. Jones, Ferenczi, Eitingon, Anna Freud, and van Ophuijsen met in Paris on 5 and 6 April 1929 for a Council meeting to discuss the issue of lay analysis and the International Psychoanalytical Association, as well as to prepare the Oxford Congress, which had been postponed to 1929 (see Schröter, 1996).
5. Signature missing.

37F

Budapest, 8th Feb[ruary] 1929[1]

Dear Ernest,

I completely agree with you that, under the circumstances, it would be entirely inappropriate to urge Mrs Rickman into an analysis.

The other question you discuss in your letter has, in the meantime, become the subject of much consideration in Vienna, where I went the weekend before last to meet Eitingon, the Professor and Anna Freud.[2] Max probably has let you know already that we Easterners consider Basel the most suitable venue for our Easter meeting. I am looking forward to seeing you again after such a long time and hope that a personal talk will serve our Cause.[3]

I thank you, on behalf of my wife too, for your interest in our well-being. The harsh winter has knocked me a bit this time, but recently I have been feeling fresher and more enthusiastic about work again. It is not impossible that the experiences and ideas of the last few years will condense themselves into a book—albeit not a very thick one.

With kind regards,

Ferenczi

Notes to letter 37F

1. Printed letterhead. The original was typewritten except for the signature.
2. Eitingon and Ferenczi were in Vienna on 25–27 January 1929. See Freud's letter to Eitingon on January 9, 1929, and Eitingon's letter to Freud on January 12, 1929 (*Freud–Eitingon, 1,* pp. 621–622). See also Ferenczi's telegram to Freud on January 25, 1929 (*Freud–Ferenczi, 3,* p. 360).
3. Ferenczi was suspicious of Jones' motives for wanting the Committee to meet in Paris rather than Basel. In a letter to Freud dated 17 February 1929, he wrote,

> I received news from Max that he and Fräulein Anna have decided on the Paris trip. I replied to Max that I will naturally come along – but at the same time I called his attention to the fact that Jones's actions in this matter are also a symptom of his other intentions. He pursues the politics of threat and brutality. If we show ourselves [to be] weak (as in the case of the matter of the trip), he will push through completely all his plans (which are, in the final analysis, purely personal–ambitious). The problem of lay analysis is for him only an excuse to unite the Anglo-Saxon world under his sceptre – I mean financially as well! (*Freud–Ferenczi, 3,* p. 363)

Freud replied on 5 March 1929,

> Be tolerant of Jones. He demands this subordination to his wishes in consideration of his 50th birthday (January 1 of this year) and the misfortune in his family, certainly childish, but hardly to be rebuffed! Giving in on this point doesn't mean that one has to acquiesce to him in all other matters. Your staying away would spoil a great deal, for the greatest tension within the former Committee does, after all, exist between you and him. (*Freud–Ferenczi, 3,* p. 364)

38F

B[uda]pest 17.II.1929.

Dear Ernest,

I hear from Max that he a[nd] Anna Freud have decided to accommodate your travel plans after all. I will, of course, bow to the majority and attend the April meeting in Paris.

With kind regards,

Sándor F.

39F

Budapest, 6th January 1930[1]

Dear Ernest,

The ambivalence of which you speak is undeniable, but the feeling is quite mutual. Your ambiguous behaviour with regard to the question of lay analysis (!) has contributed a great deal to the increase in negativity on my part.[2] Even though you yourself are president of a group with lay members, you have acted not infrequently in a manner designed to encourage the opponents of lay [analysts], e.g. at the Innsbruck Congress.[3]

The conscious mechanism behind my choice of *Festschrift*[4] topic was as follows: I was leafing through my '*Festbuch*' [for Ferenczi's 50th birthday], and found there your short paper on the link between cold and maternal care.[5] This theme then became associated with another one, which has been preoccupying me for some time and which belongs to a body of work yet to be published; I am referring to the life instinct [*Lebenstrieb*] and infantile trauma. Against the charge that, unconsciously, I wanted to offend you, there is of course no defence. Only, you too would have to ask yourself whether your interpretation might not spring from that irritability we had many an opportunity to observe in Oxford.[6]—Who might be the objective judge here? Not even Eitingon, I believe.

Thus, I am left with no other option than to return, with all due respect, the compliment of my contribution[7] being unconscious and therefore analysable (!). It may be that an effort on both sides could remove the undeniable obstacles from our path. But, seeing we are exchanging home truths, I must make a comment on your writings, too. I do not read your work with undivided pleasure either. If my papers are wild and fantastical, yours often give the impression of a kind of logical–sadistic violence, particularly since the, by the way, equally fantastical papers on child analysis appeared, I have not been enamoured with your English group at all.[8]

You see, there was enough tension in the air; perhaps this exchange of letters will mark the beginning of an improvement in our relationship.

With best wishes for the New Year from my wife and myself to you both, I remain

Your Sándor

P.S.: In all naivety, I spoke to Rickman about his motives for resigning from office[9] and hear that he did so spontaneously, was quite moved, even, by your reluctance to let him go. In no way had his resignation been urged by others. Rickman reported in a similar vein to the Professor, when he came here from London. I should like to ask for clarification in this matter, but cannot omit to mention that it might be more prudent not to write in a *Rundbrief* about the neurosis and psychosis of an analysand. I, who am familiar with the facts, have a favourable opinion of him /R./. I hope all grievances are thus done with for a long time to come, and that in future we may exchange much more monovalent letters.

Notes to letter 39F

1. Printed letterhead, henceforth: "International Psychoanalytic Association". The original was typewritten except for the salutation, the signature, and three corrections.
2. Ferenczi supplied the introduction for "The question of lay analysis" in 1926 and was, along with his Hungarian colleagues, committed to lay analysis. Ferenczi had felt for some time that Jones was unpleasantly antipathetic to him in relation to lay analysis. Freud wrote to Jones on 6 July 1927,

   > Ferenczi also expressed to me his great satisfaction with the welcome he received in London and with his stay there, regretting only that he did not obtain more far reaching agreement with you on the lay-question. You know that he fully shares my viewpoint; I know that you do not. (*Freud–Jones*, pp. 620–621)

   Reviewing Freud's book in the *International Journal*, Jones concluded that the "main argument . . . contains nothing new, it omits much of importance, and it is unmistakably partial" (Jones, 1927b, p. 92) And the Discussion on Lay Analysis that Jones published in the *International Journal* overall supported Jones' fence-sitting rather than Freud's arguments (*Int. J. Psycho-Anal.*, *8*[1927]: 174–283). Ferenczi had complained to Freud in a letter on 9 September 1929 of Jones' lack of support at the Oxford Congress: "friend Jones strove, where possible, to make even more disagreeable for us (or only for me?)" (*Freud–Ferenczi*, *3*, p. 370).
3. The Tenth Psychoanalytic Congress took place in Innsbruck from 1 to 2 September 1927. It was dominated by the topics of lay analysis and criteria for membership. There was also marked tension between Anna Freud and Melanie Klein in relation to child analysis. Eitingon was elected President. He described his impressions of Jones and Ferenczi to Freud:

   > Jones was horrid, intent always on causing annoyance, on needling one, while creating the impression that he has more still in stock, which he is keeping back to spare us. He showed me a letter from Brill, which betrays the utmost irritation and sounds as if secession were a done deal. At the same time, he credits himself with having placated them [the Americans] and kept them in the Association. A lust for evil is unmistakable; whether more or less clear intentions are involved too is difficult to say. Wolf – God only knows where animals get their instincts from – did not like him,

> laid into him and bit him. I had to punish him for it, but did so most reluctantly, because he – Jones – deserved it.
>
> I saw a lot of Ferenczi and talked with him a lot. The first time, he appeared so absent-minded that I thought his hearing might have deteriorated significantly, but this impression faded quickly. He was as accessible, kind, enthusiastic and understanding as ever. The presidential election was hardly mentioned; he readily admitted he would not have been the right man in the current circumstances. . . . Altogether, Ferenczi was a pleasure. (*Freud–Eitingon, 1*, pp. 549–550)

4. Ferenczi is referring here to his paper published in the *Zeitschrift* issue to honour Jones' 50th birthday: "Das unwillkommene Kind und sein Todestrieb" (*Zeitschrift, 15*[1929]: 149–153). The English translation ("The unwelcome child and his death-instinct") was published in the *International Journal*, 1929, see Ferenczi, 1929[287].
5. Jones (1923c) "Kälte, Krankheit und Geburt" (Cold, illness and birth) from the "*Festschrift zum 50. Geburtstag von Dr. S. Ferenczi*" (Festschrift on the 50th Birthday of Dr. S. Ferenczi).
6. Oxford was the venue for the Eleventh Psychoanalytic Congress from 27 to 31 July 1929. For details of the Congress, see Anna Freud's report in the *Zeitschrift, 17*(1929): 509–542 and *Bul. Int. Psychoanal. Assn., 10*(1929): 489–510. After the Congress, Jones was honoured by colleagues for his work on the British Medical Association Committee set up to report on psychoanalysis (see A. Freud, *Bul. Int. Psychoanal. Assn., 11*[1930]: 118–119).
7. Ferenczi seems to refer to his contribution to the ill-feeling between himself and Jones. He is also referring to his contribution to the Congress, "Fortschritte der analytischen Technik" (Developments in analytic technique), a revised version of which appeared as "Relaxationsprinzip und Neokatharsis" in the *Zeitschrift, 16*[1930]: 149–164), and with the title "The principle of relaxation and neocatharsis" in the *International Journal* (see Ferenczi, 1930[291]).
8. Ferenczi is probably referring to the papers from a Symposium held at the British Psychoanalytical Society on 4 and 18 May 1927 on child analysis, published in the *International Journal, 8*[1927]: 387–391). The Symposium was critical of Anna Freud's approach to child analysis. Ferenczi had written a foreword to the English translation of Anna Freud's *Introduction to the Technique of Child Analysis* in the translation by Pierce Clark, though when the book appeared in 1928, the foreword was omitted. In

the growing conflict over the technique appropriate to the psychoanalysis of children, Ferenczi leaned more to the side of Anna Freud than to that of his analysand, Melanie Klein. Jones inclined towards Klein. Ferenczi had complained to Freud shortly after his visit to London in 1927 about

> the prominent influence that Frau Melanie Klein has on Jones and almost the entire group. Jones is adopting not only Frau Klein's method, but also all her more personal relations to the Berlin group, etc.—Aside from the scientific value of her work, I find in this a point directed toward Vienna. Jones wanted to press me to take sides in this question as well; but I refused, and said that that was a scientific and not a partisan matter . . . (*Freud–Ferenczi, 3*, p. 313)

9. When Rickman left London for Budapest, he did not resign from his office as Secretary. He handed over his duties to Douglas Bryan in his absence. Jones had already come to rely heavily upon him administratively and pressured him to return, but, while in Budapest, Rickman wrote to him expressing grievances about the committee structure of the British Society, and his anxiety that the Institute and Clinic might be "endangered by carelessness or indifference" (Rickman to Jones, 19 September, 1929, BPAS Archives). When Rickman returned to London in 1930, some of his complaints seemed to have been responded to, but he was already considering resignation. On 23 June, his resignation from the Board and the training committee was accepted with regret (see King, 2003, pp. 20–22).

40F

International Psychoanalytic Association

Budapest, 22nd February 1930[1]

Dear Ernest,

Part of the reason for my long silence has been my wanting to wait and see, given the ambivalence you emphasise, whether I might not compose a letter of different content at a later date. Well, after all this time, I can tell you that I had few changes to make to what I would have written then. I must, however, report a change of mind in one respect, that is that on my part, too, there has been a strengthening of will and of the hope that we might, from now on, join forces and work together for our common cause without such troubles and that we might find our old, friendly tone again.

Please do send our regards to your dear wife and best wishes to you too,[2]

Notes to letter 40F

1. Printed letterhead. The original was typewritten except for the signature and a correction.
2. The signature has been cut out of the original.

41F

Dr. S. FERENCZI

BUDAPEST, I. LISZNYAI U. 11.
TELEFON 573–87

4.I.1931[1]

Dear Ernest,

I hope you will not mind that I am replying to you in German, which is more familiar to me and better suited to expressing feelings. Before all else, I should like to send our best wishes for the New Year to you and your dear wife. It would be pointless to deny that what is, after all, only a scientific, technique-related problem, that of lay analysis in America, as well as certain differences of opinion with regards to child analysis, have been the cause of a rather grim atmosphere developing between us, two old friends. Your kind letter and the pleasant surprise it was for me, seem to show that this wave of bad feeling has ebbed away in both of us; at least I no longer feel any resentment at all and am just happy, undisturbed by other tendencies inside myself, with the hope of seeing the core of the old Committee at work united. Perhaps we may draw from these events the lesson, that especially we psychoanalysts (!) should be more careful not to let scientific and scientific–technical differences degenerate into personal ones than we have been hitherto.

Said atmosphere is behind the fact that my wish to take on the presidency of the International Association has been flagging quite substantially for a time. However, the growing unity among members of council has led to a re-awakening of the old wish, so that I gave a positive answer to the Professor and Eitingon's inquiry regarding the matter.[2] I am now doing the same in relation to yours.[3]

A manifesto for my presidency is not yet relevant, at most there could, perhaps, be a re-stating of the opinion expressed already, that the undeniable scientific stagnation is in need of a certain boost.

As a lone worker, I have used these last few years of relative seclusion in an attempt to deepen theory and technique somewhat. Perhaps I will already be in a position to talk about some of this at the next congress.[4]

In any case, I hope that we will have the opportunity, during an intimate "pre-congress", to talk through the most important things and to shake hands directly, this time without a liaison officer. I am also thinking of your travelling via Budapest, where I might have the opportunity of returning the hospitality afforded to us in London in a more fitting manner than has been possible thus far. You may have heard already that I have procured a home not unlike yours /near the city but still rural/.[5] Although we do not yet have the kind of beautifully flat, English lawn in our garden which several hundred years of culturing have perfected over in your country.

Again kind regards and best wishes for the New Year from your

old Sándor

Notes to letter 41F

1. The original was typewritten except for the signature and some corrections.
2. See Freud's letter to Ferenczi on July 5, 1930, and Ferenczi's letters to Freud on July 20, 1930, and August 21, 1932. *Freud–Ferenczi, 3,* pp. 395, 396–397, 441.
3. Eitingon visited Jones in Paris on 21 September 1930 to add weight to the proposal that Ferenczi take on the presidency. Eitingon telegraphed Freud on 21 December 1930: "negotiations Jones entirely trouble-free he will propose Ferenczi himself otherwise peaceable too" (*Freud–Eitingon, 2,* pp. 706–707). In the event, Ferenczi withdrew from the possibility of becoming President in the midst of his increasingly problematic relations with Freud and members of the Committee (see Rachman, 1997).
4. The Congress, scheduled to take place in Switzerland from 7 to 10 September 1931, was cancelled due to the economic conditions. The Twelfth International Psychoanalytic Congress finally took place in Wiesbaden from 4 to 7 September 1932.
5. Ferenczi moved into his new house on 11 Lisznyai Street at the beginning of June 1930. He wrote to Freud on 25 May 1930 that it was "in a somewhat better area on the slope of the right bank of the Danube (in Buda) . . . with a garden" (*Freud–Ferenczi, 3,* p. 393).

[41aJ]

ca. end September 1932, letter missing.

[In his diary for 2 October 1932 Ferenczi wrote:][1]

(I have just received a few personally friendly lines from *Jones*. He has sent roses, suggested a circular letter.) Cannot deny that I was pleasantly touched even by this. I did indeed also feel abandoned by colleagues (Radó etc.) who are all too afraid of Freud to behave objectively or even sympathetically toward me, in case of a dispute between Freud and me. A more restrained circulation of letters between Freud, Jones, and Eitingon has certainly been going on for a long time now. I am treated like a sick person who must be spared. My interventions will have to wait until I recover, so that the special "care" becomes unnecessary.

Note to letter [41aJ]

1. Ferenczi, 1932, p. 213.

42F

DR. S. FERENCZI

BUDAPEST, I. LISZNYAI U. 11.
TELEFON: 573–87

21st Oct[ober] 1932

Dear Ernest,

Your kind parcel and your friendly lines have been a real pleasure. I cannot say that times have been particularly good lately; instead of just reacting psychically, my physical functioning has involved itself in the matter. I interrupted my holidays and came home, where I took care of myself and let myself be taken care of well, with the result that I am now able to work again.[1] Kind words from an old friend do one good under such circumstances.

The *Rundbriefe* can or could do some good, if everyone were to communicate in all honesty through them.

My wife thanks yours for the beautiful and kind letter; I happily join her in this.

With kind regards,

Sándor

Note to letter 42F

1. Despite vehement opposition from Freud, Ferenczi gave his paper "Die Leidenschaften der Erwachsenen und deren Einfluß auf Sexual- und Charakterentwicklung der Kinder" (Adult passions and their influence on children's sexual and character development) at the Wiesbaden Congress on 4 September 1932. It was published as "Sprachverwirrung zwischen den Erwachsenen und dem Kind" ("Confusion of tongues between the adults and the child") in the Zeitschrift, 19 (Ferenczi, 1933[294]). Ferenczi was deeply shaken by his last visit to Freud prior to the Congress. When, after their talk, he extended his hand to Freud for a friendly goodbye, Freud turned his back on him. He wrote to Freud from Luchon in the South of France on 27 September:

> You can measure by the length of the reaction time the depth of the shock with which our conversation in Vienna before the Congress came to me. Unfortunately, such things are always connected to bodily ailments in me, so that my trip to the south of France by way of Baden-Baden was and is, actually, a "voyage de lit-à-lit". (*Freud–Ferenczi, 3,* p. 443)

Ferenczi had to interrupt his holidays following the Congress and return home to Budapest. He was suffering from pernicious anaemia and never recovered. Jones was convinced that Ferenczi was psychologically as well as physically ill. On 9 September 1932, he wrote to Freud,

> In the first place will you allow me to express my sympathy over the difficulty that has arisen with your oldest and dearest analytical friend. . . . Nevertheless, how painful it must be I can imagine. To Eitingon it came as a shock of surprise, to you probably less so. To me not at all, for I have followed F[erenczi]'s evolution (including the pathological side) for many years, and knew it could only be a question of time before his denouement arrived. Abraham and I drew him forcibly back from the precipice at the Rank time, and lately Rickman's regular reports of his analysis showed me clearly the direction things were going. His exceptionally deep need of being loved, together with the repressed sadism, are plainly behind the tendency to ideas of persecution. My reaction was therefore very simple: first the Cause, then everything to keep him with us. The first excluded the possibility of his being president . . . [Eitingon and Van Ophuijsen] wanted at all cost that Ferenczi be asked to withdraw his Vortrag and to postpone as long

> as possible the expression of his ideas – to avoid scandal. On the contrary I insisted that it would be less scandal if we kept it inside the Vereinigung and that we were quite strong enough to digest the ideas ourselves without harm coming. It would have fed the pathological ideas to have told him that his Vortrag etc. was too wicked to be presented to us. . . . He is, I am afraid, a sick man – also physically – and the impression he made was very pathetic. To me personally he was affectionate, and I think I was able to help both him and his wife. It is terrible – but also unprofitable – to make comparisons with the brilliant past. (*Freud–Jones*, pp. 706–707)

For a detailed account of the pressure on Ferenczi not to read his paper, including Freud's response when Ferenczi read it to him in Vienna three days before the Congress, see Rachman, 1997. In addition, for Jones' allegations about Ferenczi's health, repeated in his biography of Freud, see Bonomi, 1998.

43F

DR. S. FERENCZI

BUDAPEST, I. LISZNYAI U. 11.
TELEFON: 573–87

March 22, 1933[1]

Dear Ernest,

I do not feel inclined to suggest any alterations on the paper Alexander[2] wants to publish in the April number of his Journal.[3] At the same time I thank you for wanting to publish my Congress paper[4] in the English Journal. As to your question about winter and spring, I have to tell you that I had a rather trying winter but am looking forward to spring hopefully.

Your roses[5] seem to have endured the winter rather nicely, at least I hope so because the winter season was rather mild.

I hope the roses will often remind me of both you and your beautiful country-place.

Cordially greetings from yours

Ferenczi

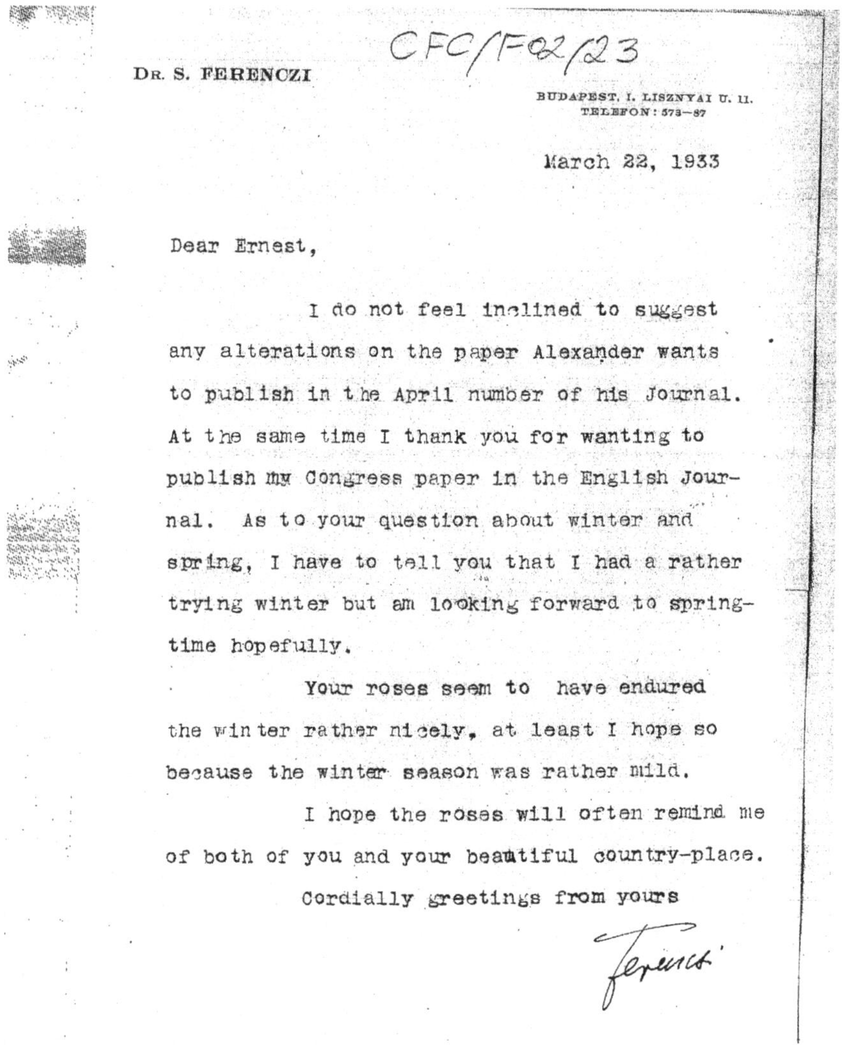

CFC/F02/23

DR. S. FERENCZI

BUDAPEST, I. LISZNYAI U. 11.
TELEFON: 573–87

March 22, 1933

Dear Ernest,

I do not feel inclined to suggest any alterations on the paper Alexander wants to publish in the April number of his Journal. At the same time I thank you for wanting to publish my Congress paper in the English Journal. As to your question about winter and spring, I have to tell you that I had a rather trying winter but am looking forward to springtime hopefully.

Your roses seem to have endured the winter rather nicely, at least I hope so because the winter season was rather mild.

I hope the roses will often remind me of both of you and your beautiful country-place.

Cordially greetings from yours

Ferenczi

Letter from Ferenczi to Jones, March 22, 1933.

Notes to letter 43F

1. The original is typewritten except for the signature. It was probably typed by Elma Pálos.
2. Franz Gabriel Alexander (1891–1964) was a psychiatrist and the "father of psychoanalytic psychosomatics". He was born in Budapest as the son

of the well-known Hungarian philosopher, Bernát Alexander. He obtained his medical degree in 1913. In 1919, he was an assistant at the neurological clinic of the Medical Faculty of the Budapest University. In 1920, he moved to Berlin to enter analysis with Hanns Sachs, become the first candidate of the Berlin Psychoanalytic Institute, and, later, one of its training analysts and teachers. He emigrated to the United States in the autumn of 1930. From 1932 to 1953, he served as head of the Chicago Institute of Psychoanalysis and became the first American Professor of Psychoanalysis. In 1939, he founded the journal *Psychosomatic Medicine*.

3. The paper cannot be clearly identified. Ferenczi's "Thalassa: a theory of genitality" appeared in *Psychoanalytic Quarterly* in instalments from 1933 to 1936 (*Psychoanal Q.* 1933, *2*: 361–403; 1934, *3*: 1–29, 200–222; 1936, *5*: 249–260), but the first instalment was announced and published after Ferenczi's death and it is not clear in what sense *Psychoanalytic Quarterly* could be said to be Alexander's journal. *Psychoanalytic Quarterly* was associated with the New York Society, not Chicago, being founded in 1932 as its organ. Alexander's *Psychosomatic Medicine* started in 1939. *The Journal of Nervous and Mental Diseases* was published from Chicago and Alexander's (and Menninger's) "The relation of persecutory delusions to the functioning of the gastro-intestinal tract" appeared in it in 1936 (*85*: 541–554). Again, however, it was not Alexander's journal.
4. Ferenczi refers to his 1932 paper "Sprachverwirrung zwischen den Erwachsenen und dem Kind. (Die Sprache der Zärtlichkeit und der Leidenschaft)" ("Confusion of tongues between the adults and the child. (The language of tenderness and passion)"), read at the Wiesbaden Congress and published in the *Zeitschrift*, *19*(1933): 5–15. Ferenczi's death on 24 May 1933 relieved Jones of his undertaking to publish his controversial paper. In a letter to Freud dated 3 June 1933, Jones wrote of his decision not to publish:

> I hoped that Ferenczi himself would not publish it, but when I received the proofs of the *ZEITSCHRIFT* I felt he would be offended if it were not translated into English and so asked his permission for this. He seemed gratified, and we have not only translated it but set it up in type as the first paper in the July number. Since his death I have been thinking over the removal of the personal reason for publishing it. Others also have suggested that it now be withdrawn and I quote the following passage from a letter of Mrs. Riviere's, [with] which I quite agree: "Now that Ferenczi has died, I wondered whether you will not reconsider publishing his last paper. It seems to me it can only be damaging

> to him and a discredit, while now that he is no longer to be hurt by its not being published, no good purpose could be served by it. Its scientific contentions and its statements about analytic practice are just a tissue of delusions, which can only discredit psa. and give credit to its opponents. It cannot be supposed that all *JOURNAL* readers will appreciate the mental condition of the writer, and in this respect one has to think of posterity too! I therefore think it best to withdraw the paper unless I hear from you that you have any wish to the contrary. (*Freud–Jones*, p. 722)

5. Jones was fond of his "wonderful rose garden" (*Freud–Jones*, p. 675) and must have sent Ferenczi rose bushes to plant in his new garden. Ferenczi would have seen Jones's rose garden when he visited him at the Plat. These may be the roses (rose bushes) referred to in Jones' missing letter from ca. September 1932.

APPENDIX

The Ferenczi–Jones correspondence

Entries in italics refer to letters solely between Ferenczi and Jones, except for 11 April 1914. Those in square brackets, also in italics, represent missing letters to which a date may reasonably be attached. Other entries refer to *Rundbriefe* by the two men which contain passages addressed more or less directly to each other.

Ferenczi	*8 April 1911*
Ferenczi	*14 November 1911*
Ferenczi	*[ca 6 November 1912]*
Ferenczi	*25 September 1913*
Ferenczi	*25 October 1913*
Ferenczi	*2 November 1913*
Ferenczi	*8 November 1913*
Ferenczi	*16 December 1913*
Ferenczi	*16 March 1914*
Ferenczi	*11 April 1914 (with Freud and Rank)*
Ferenczi	*20 May 1914*
Ferenczi	*20 May 1914 (with Radó)*
Ferenczi	*23 June 1914*
Ferenczi	*[20 July 1914]*

Ferenczi	*26 July 1914*
Ferenczi	*29 July 1914*
Ferenczi	*15 May 1915*
Ferenczi	*[ca 24 July 1916]*
Ferenczi	20 September 1920 (*Die Rundbriefe, 1*: 52)
Jones	*7 October 1920 (Die Rundbriefe, 1: 71–72)*
Ferenczi	18 October 1920 (*Die Rundbriefe, 1*: 90–91)
Ferenczi	24 October 1920 (*Die Rundbriefe, 1*: 114–115)
Jones	26 October 1920 (*Die Rundbriefe, 1*: 116–117)
Ferenczi	30 October 1920 (*Die Rundbriefe, 1*: 137)
Jones	2 November 1920 (*Die Rundbriefe, 1*: 140)
Ferenczi	7 November 1920 (*Die Rundbriefe, 1*:, 157–158)
Jones	9 November 1920 (*Die Rundbriefe, 1*: 159)
Ferenczi	25 November 1920 (*Die Rundbriefe, 1*: 190)
Jones	30 November 1920 (*Die Rundbriefe, 1*: 191)
Ferenczi	6 December 1920 (*Die Rundbriefe, 1*: 201)
Jones	7 December 1920 (*Die Rundbriefe, 1*: 202)
Ferenczi	14 December 1920 (*Die Rundbriefe, 1*: 212)
Jones	15 December 1920 (*Die Rundbriefe, 1*: 221)
Jones	21 December 1920 (*Die Rundbriefe, 1*: 222)
Ferenczi	21 December 1920 (*Die Rundbriefe, 1*: 226)
Jones	31 December 1920 (*Die Rundbriefe, 1*: 241–242)
Ferenczi	1 January 1921 (*Die Rundbriefe*, 2: 15–16)
Jones	11 January 1921 (*Die Rundbriefe*, 2: 25)
Ferenczi	11 January 1921 (*Die Rundbriefe*, 2: 29)
Ferenczi	21 January 1921 (*Die Rundbriefe*, 2: 39–40)
Jones	21 January 1921 (*Die Rundbriefe*, 2: 41)
Jones	1 February 1921 (*Die Rundbriefe*, 2: 52)
Ferenczi	2 February 1921 (*Die Rundbriefe*, 2: 56)
Ferenczi	11 February 1921 (*Die Rundbriefe*, 2: 65)
Jones	11 February 1921 (*Die Rundbriefe*, 2: 68)
Ferenczi	21 February 1921 (*Die Rundbriefe*, 2: 83)
Jones	21 February 1921 (*Die Rundbriefe*, 2: 85)
Ferenczi	2 March 1921 (*Die Rundbriefe*, 2: 102)
Ferenczi	11 March 1921 (*Die Rundbriefe*, 2: 109)
Jones	11 March 1921 (*Die Rundbriefe*, 2: 111)
Jones	21 March 1921 (*Die Rundbriefe*, 2: 121)
Ferenczi	22 March 1921 (*Die Rundbriefe*, 2: 125–126)
Ferenczi	1 April 1921 (*Die Rundbriefe*, 2: 131)

Jones	1 April 1921 (*Die Rundbriefe*, 2: 133)
Ferenczi	11 April 1921 (*Die Rundbriefe*, 2: 140)
Jones	11 April 1921 (*Die Rundbriefe*, 2: 142)
Ferenczi	22 April 1921 (*Die Rundbriefe*, 2: 147)
Ferenczi	1 May 1921 (*Die Rundbriefe*, 2: 152)
Jones	11 May 1921 (*Die Rundbriefe*, 2:, 158)
Ferenczi	12 May 1921 (*Die Rundbriefe*, 2: 162)
Jones	21 May 1921 (*Die Rundbriefe*, 2: 171–172)
Ferenczi	1 June 1921 (*Die Rundbriefe*, 2: 180)
Jones	11 June 1921 (*Die Rundbriefe*, 2: 192)
[Ferenczi	*12 June 1921]*
Ferenczi	12 June 1921 (*Die Rundbriefe*, 2: 195)
Ferenczi	21 June 1921 (*Die Rundbriefe*, 2: 201–202)
Jones	21 June 1921 (*Die Rundbriefe*, 2: 204)
Jones	1 July 1921 (*Die Rundbriefe*, 2: 212)
Ferenczi	3 July 1921 (*Die Rundbriefe*, 2: 214)
Ferenczi	11 July 1921
Jones	22 July 1921 (*Die Rundbriefe*, 2: 224)
[*Jones*	*12 August 1921 (enclosed with Rundbrief: Die Rundbriefe,* 2: 231)]
Jones	21 October 1921 (*Die Rundbriefe*, 2: 259)
Ferenczi	3 November 1921 (*Die Rundbriefe*, 2: 271)
Ferenczi	11 November 1921 (*Die Rundbriefe*, 2: 275)
Jones	11 November 1921 (*Die Rundbriefe*, 2: 277)
Ferenczi	1 December 1921 (*Die Rundbriefe*, 2: 295–296)
Jones	1 December 1921 (*Die Rundbriefe*, 2: 298)
Ferenczi	11 December 1921 (*Die Rundbriefe*, 2: 309)
Jones	11 December 1921 (*Die Rundbriefe*, 2: 310–311)
Ferenczi	21 December 1921 (*Die Rundbriefe*, 2: 317)
Jones	21 December 1921 (*Die Rundbriefe*, 2: 320)
Jones	11 January 1922 (*Die Rundbriefe*, 3: 19)
Ferenczi	*22 January 1922*
Jones	31 January 1922 (*Die Rundbriefe*, 3: 36–37)
Jones	11 February 1922 (*Die Rundbriefe*, 3: 52)
Ferenczi	12 February 1922 (*Die Rundbriefe*, 3: 57)
Ferenczi	20 February 1922
Ferenczi	21 February 1922 (*Die Rundbriefe*, 3: 66)
Jones	21 February 1922 (*Die Rundbriefe*, 3: 69)
Ferenczi	1 March 1922 (*Die Rundbriefe*, 3: 75)

Jones	2 March 1922 (*Die Rundbriefe*, 3: 78)
Ferenczi	15 March 1922 (*Die Rundbriefe*, 3: 91)
[*Jones*	*1 April 1922 (enclosed with Rundbrief: Die Rundbriefe, 3: 106)*]
Ferenczi	17 April 1922 (*Die Rundbriefe*, 3: 115)
Jones	19 April 1922 (*Die Rundbriefe*, 3: 118–119)
Jones	15 May 1922 (*Die Rundbriefe*, 3: 141)
Ferenczi	17 May 1922 (*Die Rundbriefe*, 3: 148)
Jones	1 June 1922 (*Die Rundbriefe*, 3: 154)
Ferenczi	2 June 1922 (*Die Rundbriefe*, 3: 159)
Ferenczi	14 June 1922 (*Die Rundbriefe*, 3: 164)
Ferenczi and Rank	*1 August 1922 (Die Rundbriefe, 3: 187–188)*
Ferenczi	22 October 1922
Ferenczi	30 October 1922 (*Die Rundbriefe*, 3: 212–213)
Jones	16 November 1922 (*Die Rundbriefe*: 3, 229)
Jones	11 January 1923 (*Die Rundbriefe*, 4: 23)
Ferenczi	15 January 1923 (*Die Rundbriefe*, 4: 27–28)
Jones	1 February 1923 (*Die Rundbriefe*, 4: 36–37)
Ferenczi	8 February 1923 (*Die Rundbriefe*, 4: 41)
Jones	15 February 1923 (*Die Rundbriefe*, 4: 42)
Ferenczi	1 March 1923 (*Die Rundbriefe*, 4: 57)
Ferenczi	17 March 1923 (*Die Rundbriefe*, 4: 67)
Ferenczi	30 March 1923 (*Die Rundbriefe*, 4: 71)
Jones	5 April 1923 (*Die Rundbriefe*, 4: 76–77)
Ferenczi	1 May 1923 (*Die Rundbriefe*, 4: 83)
Jones	1 May 1923 (*Die Rundbriefe*, 4: 84)
Jones	15 June 1923 (*Die Rundbriefe*, 4: 97)
Ferenczi	*6 July 1923*
Ferenczi	*7 October 1923*
Ferenczi	2 November 1923 (*Die Rundbriefe*, 4: 121–122)
Jones	12 November 1923 (*Die Rundbriefe*, 4: 127–130)
Ferenczi	2 December 1923 (*Die Rundbriefe*, 4: 137–138)
Jones	2 December 1923 (*Die Rundbriefe*, 4: 140)
Jones	15 December 1923 (*Die Rundbriefe*, 4: 144)
[*Jones*	*15 December 1923 (enclosed with Rundbrief: DieRundbriefe, 4:144)*]
Ferenczi	*13 January 1924*
Ferenczi	13 January 1924 (*Die Rundbriefe*, 4: 151–152)

Jones	15 January 1924 (*Die Rundbriefe*, 4: 153)
Jones	2 February 1924 (*Die Rundbriefe*, 4: 162)
Ferenczi	*10 April 1924*
Jones	*7 August 1924*
Ferenczi	*18 August 1924*
[*Jones*	*4 October 1924 (see above letter)*]
Ferenczi	*12 October 1924*
Ferenczi	15 December 1924 (*Die Rundbriefe*, 4: 204)
Ferenczi	17 January 1925 (*Die Rundbriefe*, 4: 229–230)
Jones	16 March 1925 (*Die Rundbriefe*, 4: 249–250)
Ferenczi	*29 May 1925*
Jones	*5 June 1925*
Jones	19 November 1925 (*Die Rundbriefe*, 4: 285)
Ferenczi	13 April 1926 (*Die Rundbriefe*, 4: 310)
Jones	22 June 1926 (*Die Rundbriefe*, 4: 316)
Ferenczi	25 July 1926 (*Die Rundbriefe*, 4: 320)
Jones	30 July 1926 (*Die Rundbriefe*, 4: 322)
Jones	16 September 1926 (*Die Rundbriefe*, 4: 324)
Jones	*5 October 1926*
Jones	15 November 1926 (*Die Rundbriefe*, 4: 326)
Jones	13 December 1926
Jones	16 December 1926 (*Die Rundbriefe*, 4: 336)
Jones	17 January 1927 (*Die Rundbriefe*, 4: 341)
Ferenczi	26 February 1927 (*Die Rundbriefe*, 4: 359)
Ferenczi	21 March 1927 (*Die Rundbriefe*, 4: 362)
Ferenczi	*26 June 1927*
Jones	*1 February 1929*
Ferenczi	*8 February 1929*
Ferenczi	17 February 1929
Ferenczi	*6 July 1929*
Ferenczi	*6 January 1930*
Ferenczi	*22 February 1930*
Ferenczi	4 January 1931
[*Jones*	*ca. 20 August 1932*]
Ferenczi	*21 October 1932*
Ferenczi	22 March 1933

REFERENCES

Adler, A. (1911). Beitrag zur Lehre vom Widerstand (Contribution to the theory of resistance). *Zentralblatt für Psychoanalyse: Medizinische Monatsschrift für Seelenkunde, 1*: 214–219.

Alexander, F. (1925). Entwicklungsziele der Psychoanalyse. By S. Ferenczi & O. Rank (1924). (Neue Arbeiten zur ärztlichen Psychoanalyse (New works on medical psychoanalysis), Nr. I). *International Journal of Psychoanalysis, 6*: 484–496.

Andreas-Salomé, L. (1964). *The Freud Journal*. S. A. Leavy (Trans.). New York: Basic Books.

Avello, J. J. (1998). Metapsychology in Ferenczi: death instinct or death passion? *International Forum of Psychoanalysis, 7*: 229–233.

Bacciagaluppi, M. (1994). The influence of Ferenczi on Bowlby. *International Forum of Psychoanalysis, 3*: 97–101.

Bleuler, E. (1911). Alkohol und Neurosen. *Jahrbuch für psychoanalytische und psychopathologische Forschungen, 3*: 848–852.

Bleuler, E. (1913). Die Kritik der Freudschen Theorie. *Allgemeine Zeitschrift für Psychiatrie und psychisch gerichtliche Medizin, 70*: 665–718.

Bleuler, E. (1916). *Lehrbuch der Psychiatrie*. Berlin: J. Springer, 1916. English edn, *Textbook of Psychiatry*, A. A. Brill (Trans.). New York: Macmillan, 1924 [reprinted New York: Arno Press, 1976].

Bókay, A. (1998). Turn of fortune in psychoanalysis: the 1924 Rank debates and the origins of hermeneutic psychoanalysis. *International Forum of Psychoanalysis*, 7: 189–199.

Bonomi, C. (1998). Jones's allegation of Ferenczi's mental deterioration. *International Forum of Psychoanalysis*, 7: 201–206.

Bos, J., & Groenendijk, L. (2007). *The Self-Marginalization of Wilhelm Stekel. Freudian Circles Inside and Out*. New York: Springer-Verlag.

Bowlby, J. (1988). Foreword. In: I. D. Suttie, *The Origins of Love and Hate* (xv–xviii). London: Free Association Books.

Bradley, N. (2002). Response: Karin Stephen, the superego and internal objects. *Psychoanalysis and History*, 4: 225–230.

Brome, V. (1983). *Ernest Jones: Freud's Alter Ego*. New York: Norton.

Cassullo, G. (2010). Back to the roots: the influence of Ian D. Suttie on British psychoanalysis. *American Imago*, 67: 5–22.

Cole, E. M. (1922). A few "don'ts" for beginners in the technique of psycho-analysis. *International Journal of Psychoanalysis*, 3: 43–44.

Cole, E. M. (1928). *Three Minute Talks About Children*. London: C. W. Daniel.

Erős, F. (2010). Gender, hysteria and war neurosis. In: A. Schwartz (Ed.), *Gender and Modernity in Central Europe. The Austro-Hungarian Legacy* (pp. 185–201). Ottawa: University of Ottawa Press.

Erős, F. (2011). *Pszichoanalízis és forradalom*. Ferenczi Sándor és a budapesti egyetem 1918/19-ben (Sándor Ferenczi and the University of Budapest in 19188–19). Budapest: Jószöveg Műhely Kiadó.

Falzeder, E. (Ed.) (2002). *The Complete Correspondence of Sigmund Freud and Karl Abraham, 1907–1925*. London: Karnac.

Falzeder, E., & Brabant, E. (Eds.) (1994). *The Correspondence of Sigmund Freud and Sándor Ferenczi, Volume 1, 1908–1914*, P. T. Hoffer (Trans.). Cambridge, MA: Harvard University Press.

Falzeder, E., & Brabant, E. (Eds.) (1996). *The Correspondence of Sigmund Freud and Sándor Ferenczi, Volume 2, 1914–1919*, P. T. Hoffer (Trans.). Cambridge, MA: Harvard University Press.

Falzeder, E., & Brabant, E. (Eds.) (2000). *The Correspondence of Sigmund Freud and Sándor Ferenczi, Volume 3, 1920–1933*, P. T. Hoffer (Trans.). Cambridge, MA: Harvard University Press.

Falzeder, E. M., & Burnham, J. C. (2007). A perfectly staged 'concerted action' against psychoanalysis: the 1913 congress of German psychiatrists. *International Journal of Psychoanalysis*, 88: 1223–1244.

Ferenczi, S. (1909[67]). Introjektion und Übertragung. In: *Schriften zur Psychoanalyse I* (pp. 12–47), 1970[313]. Introjection and transference. In: *Contributions to Psychoanalysis* (pp. 35–93), 1916[186].

Ferenczi, S. (1911[80]). Über die Rolle der Homosexualität in der Pathogenese der Paranoia. In: *Schriften zur Psychoanalyse I* (pp. 73–91), 1970[313]. On the part played by homosexuality in the pathogenesis of paranoia. In: *Contributions to Psychoanalysis* (pp. 154–186), 1916[186].

Ferenczi, S. (1911[81]). Alkohol und Neurosen. Antwort auf eine Kritik des Herrn Professor E. Bleuler [Alcohol and neurosis. A reply to the criticisms of Prof. Eugen Bleuler]. In: *Schriften zur Psychoanalyse I* (pp. 92–96), 1970[313].

Ferenczi, S. (1912[94]). The psycho-analysis of suggestion and hypnosis (Trans. A. Newbold). *Transaction of the Psycho-Medical Society*, *3*(4): 3–11.

Ferenczi, S. (1913[111]). Stages in the development of the sense of reality. In: *Contributions to Psychoanalysis* (pp. 213–239). Boston, MA: R. G. Badger.

Ferenczi, S. (1913[124]). Kritik der Jungschen *Wandlungen und Symbole der Libido* (A critque of Jung's Transformations and Symbolisms of the Libido). *Internationale Zeitschrift für ärztliche Psychoanalyse*, *1*: 391–403 [reprinted in: *Bausteine zur Psychoanalyse, Volume 1* (pp. 243–268), 1927].

Ferenczi, S. (1914[136]). Zur Nosologie der männlichen Homosexualität (Homoerotik). *Internationale Zeitschrift für ärztliche Psychoanalyse*, *2*: 131–142. On the nosology of male homosexuality (homo-erotism). In: *Contributions to Psychoanalysis* (pp. 296–328), 1916[186].

Ferenczi, S. (1914[149]). *Ideges tünetek keletkezése és eltűnése és egyéb értekezések a pszichoanalízis köréből* (Origin and disappearance of neurotic symptoms, and other treatises on psycho-analysis). Budapest: Dick Manó, 1914, 1919, 1922.

Ferenczi, S. (1914[150]). Referatum Prof. E. Bleuler. "Kritik der Freudschen Theorie". *Internationale Zeitschrift für ärztliche Psychoanalyse*, *2*:62–66 [reprinted in: *Bausteine zur Psychoanalyse, Volume 4* (pp. 54–64), 1938].

Ferenczi, S. (1914[no regist.]). A pszichoanalízisről és annak jogi és társadalmi jelentőségéről (On psychoanalysis and its significance to society and the law). *Gyógyászat*, *54*(6): 88–91.

Ferenczi, S. (1916[186]). *Contributions to Psychoanalysis*. E. Jones (Trans.). Boston, MA: R. G. Badger [reprinted in *First Contributions to Psycho-Analysis*, London: Hogarth Press, 1952; London: Karnac, 1980, 1994].

Ferenczi, S. (1917[199]). Barátságom Schächter Miksával (My friendship with Max Schächter). *Gyógyászat*, *57*(52):26–27 [reprinted in *Thalassa* (Budapest), 1992, *3*(2):140–143].

Ferenczi, S. (1921[232]). Psychoanalytische Betrachtungen über den Tic. *Schriften zur Psychoanalyse II* (pp. 39–69). Psychoanalytic considerations regarding the tic. *Further Contributions to the Theory and Technique of Psycho-Analysis* (pp. 142–174).

Ferenczi, S. (1922[244]). Freuds 'Massenpsychologie und Ich-Analyse': Der individualpsychologische Fortschritt. *Schriften zur Psychoanalyse II* (pp. 122–126). Freud's 'Group psychology and the analysis of the ego': Its contributions to the psychology of the individual. *Final Contributions to the Problems and Methods of Psycho-Analysis* (pp. 371–376), 1955.

Ferenczi, S. (1924[267]). Ignotus, a megértő [Ignotus, the understanding]. *Nyugat, 17* (1924), no. 23.

Ferenczi, S. (1924[268]). *Versuch einer Genitaltheorie.* Leipzig: Internationaler Psychoanalytischer Verlag. *Thalassa; Theory of Genitality.* Albany, NY: The Psychoanalytic Quarterly, 1938 [reprinted London: Karnac, 1990].

Ferenczi, S. (1926[276]). *Further Contributions to the Theory and Technique of Psycho-Analysis.* Compiled by John Rickman. J. I. Suttie & others (Trans.). London: Hogarth Press, 1926 (2nd edition, 1950) [reprinted, London: Karnac, 1980, 1994].

Ferenczi, S. (1927[277]). O. Rank: *Technik Der Psychoanalyse*: I. Die Analytische Situation. *Internationale Zeitschrift für ärztliche Psychoanalyse, 13*: 1–9 [reprinted entitled Zur Kritik der Rankschen *Technik Der Psychoanalyse.* In: *Bausteine zur Psychoanalyse, Volume 2* (pp. 116–128), 1927]. Technik Der Psychoanalyse: I. Die Analytische Situation. By Dr. Otto Rank (1926). *International Journal of Psychoanalysis, 8*: 93–100.

Ferenczi, S. (1928[281]). The adaptation of the family to the child: being free-associations on children's education. *British Journal of Medical Psychology, 8*(1): 1–13 [reprinted in: *Final Contributions to the Problems and Methods of Psycho-Analysis* (pp. 61–76), 1955].

Ferenczi, S. (1929[287]). Das unwillkommene Kind und sein Todestrieb. *Internationale Zeitschrift für ärztliche Psychoanalyse, 15*:149–153 [reprinted in: *Schriften zur Psychoanalyse II* (pp. 251–256), 1970]. The unwelcome child and his death-instinct. *International Journal of Psychoanalysis, 10*: 125–129 [reprinted in: *Final Contributions to the Problems and Methods of Psycho-Analysis* (pp. 102–107), 1955].

Ferenczi, S. (1930[291]). Relaxationsprinzip und Neokatharsis. *Internationale Zeitschrift für ärztliche Psychoanalyse, 16*:149–164 [reprinted in: *Schriften zur Psychoanalyse II* (pp. 257–273), 1970]. The principle of relaxation and neocatharsis. *International Journal of Psychoanalysis, 11*: 428–443 [reprinted in: *Final Contributions to the Problems and Methods of Psycho-Analysis* (pp. 108–125), 1955].

Ferenczi, S. (1932). *The Clinical Diary of Sándor Ferenczi*, J. Dupont (Ed.), M. Balint and N. Z. Jackson (Trans.). Cambridge, MA: Harvard University Press, 1988.

Ferenczi, S. (1933[294]). Sprachverwirrung zwischen den Erwachsenen und dem Kind (Die Sprache der Zärtlichkeit und der Leidenschaft). *Internationale Zeitschrift für ärztliche Psychoanalyse, 19*: 5–15 [reprinted in: *Schirften zur Psychoanalyse II* (pp. 303–313), 1970]. Confusion of tongues between the adults and the child (The language of tenderness and of passion). *International Journal of Psychoanalysis, 30*: 225–230 [reprinted in: *Final Contributions to the Problems and Methods of Psycho-Analysis* (pp. 256–267), 1955].

Ferenczi, S. (1988). *The Clinical Diary of Sándor Ferenczi*, J. Dupont (Ed.), M. Balint & N. Zarday Jackson (Trans.). Cambridge, MA: Harvard University Press [reprinted, 1995].

Ferenczi, S., & Groddeck, G. (2006). *Briefwechsel Sándor Ferenczi – George Groddeck*, M. Giefer (Ed.). Frankfurt: Stroemfeld Verlag.

Ferenczi, S., & Hollós, S. (István) (1922[239]). *Zur Psychoanalyse der paralytischen Geistesstörungen*. Wien/Leipzig: Internationaler Psychoanalytischer Verlag. English edn, *Psychoanalysis and the Psychic Disorders of General Paresis*. New York: Nervous and Mental Disease Publishing, 1925.

Ferenczi, S., & Rank, O. (1924). *Entwicklungsziele der Psychoanalyse: Zur Wechselbeziehung von Theorie und Praxis*. Leipzig: Internationaler Psychoanalytischer Verlag, 1924. English edn, *The Development of Psychoanalysis*. New York: Nervous and Mental Disease Publishing, 1925 [reprinted Madison, CT: International Universities Press, 1986].

Fortune, C. (Ed.) (2002). *The Sándor Ferenczi–George Groddeck Correspondence 1921–1933*. London: Open Gate Press.

Franklin, M. E. (1928). Die bedingten Reflexe bei Epilepsie und der Wiederholungszwang (Conditional reflexes in epilepsy and the repetition compulsion). *Imago, 14*: 364–376.

Franklin, M. E. (1933). Family reactions during the analysis of a case of obsessional neurosis. *International Journal of Psychoanalysis, 14*: 87–107.

Freud, E. L. (Ed.) (1961). *Letters of Sigmund Freud 1873–1939*. London: Hogarth Press.

Freud, S. (1900a). *The Interpretation of Dreams*. *S.E., 5*. London: Hogarth.

Freud, S. (1908a). Hysterical phantasies and their relation to bisexuality. *S.E., 9*: 155–166. London: Hogarth.

Freud, S, (1908f). Preface to Wilhelm Stekel's *Nervous Anxiety-States and their Treatment*. *S.E., 9*: 250–251. London: Hogarth.

Freud, S. (1910a). Five lectures on psycho-analysis. *S.E., 11*: 7–55. London: Hogarth.

Freud, S. (1912f). Contributions to a discussion on masturbation. *S.E., 12*: pp. 239–254. London: Hogarth.

Freud, S. (1914c). On narcissism. An introduction. *S.E., 14*: 73–102. London: Hogarth.

Freud, S. (1914d). On the history of the psycho-analytic movement. *S.E., 14*: 3–66. London: Hogarth.

Freud, S. (1919j). On the teaching of psycho-analysis in universities. *S.E., 17*: 169–174. London: Hogarth.

Freud, S. (1926e). The question of lay analysis. Conversations with an impartial person. *S.E., 20*: 183–250. London: Hogarth.

Giampieri, P., & Erős, F. (1987). The beginnings of the reception of psychoanalysis in Hungary, 1900–1920. *Sigmund Freud House Bulletin, 11*(2): 13–27.

Glover, E. (1924). 'Active therapy' and psycho-analysis—a critical review. *International Journal of Psychoanalysis, 5*: 269–311.

Glover, E. (1927). Further Contributions to the Theory and Technique of Psycho-Analysis: by Sándor Ferenczi, M.D. *International Journal of Psychoanalysis, 8*: 417–421.

Glover, E. (1927–1928). Lectures on technique in psycho-analysis [I–VIII]. *International Journal of Psychoanalysis, 8*: 311–338; 486–520; *International Journal of Psychoanalysis*, 9: 7–46; 181–218.

Grosskurth, P. (1986). *Melanie Klein. Her World and Her Work.* London: Hodder and Stoughton.

Grosskurth, P. (1991). *The Secret Ring: Freud's Inner Circle and the Politics of Psychoanalysis.* London: Jonathan Cape.

Gutheil, E. A. (Ed.) (1950). *The Autobiography of Wilhelm Stekel: The Life Story Of a Pioneer Psychoanalyst.* New York: Liveright.

Hale, N. G. Jr. (Ed.) (1971). *James Jackson Putnam and Psychoanalysis. Letters Between Putnam and Sigmund Freud, Ernest Jones, William James, Sandor Ferenczi, and Morton Prince, 1877–1917.* Cambridge, MA: Harvard University Press.

Herford (Budgett-Meakin), E. (1928). The infantile mind and its relations to social problems and mental hygiene. *Journal of State Medicine, 36*: 139–148.

Hermann, I. (1976[1935]). Clinging—going-in-search—a contrasting pair of instincts and their relation to sadism and masochism. *Psychoanalytic Quarterly, 45*: 5–36.

Hitschmann, E. (1913). *Freud's Theories of the Neuroses.* New York: The Journal of Nervous and Mental Disease Publishing.

Hollós, I. (1927). *Búcsúm a Sárga Háztól: Dr. Pfeiflein Telemach különös írása az elmebetegek felszabadításáról* (Behind the yellow wall: on the liberation of the lunatic). Budapest: Genius, 1927 [reprinted, Budapest: Cserépfalvi, 1990]. *Hinter der gelben Mauer: von der Befreiung des Irren.* Stuttgart: Hippokrates Verlag, 1928. Mes adieux à la Maison jaune. *Le Coq-Héron*, No. 100, 1986.

Hollós, I. (1974). Brief eines Entronnenen (Letter of an escapee). Istvan Hollos an Paul Federn (17.02.1946) (Aus dem Archiv der Psychoanalyse). *Psyche, 28*(3): 266–268.

Ignotus (Veigelsberg, H.) (1933). Búcsúztató. *Magyar Hírlap, 43*(120): 5, (28 May 1933). Eulogy by Ignotus, M. Baczoni (Trans.). In: J. Szekacs-Weisz & T. Keve (Eds.), *Ferenczi and His World: Rekindling the Spirit of the Budapest School* (pp. 2–6). London: Karnac, 2012.

Inman, W. S. (1958). Clinical thought-reading. *International Journal of Psychoanalysis, 39*: 386–396.

Jones, E. (1910a). The therapeutic effect of suggestion. *Canadian Journal of Medicine and Surgery, 29*(1910[August]): 78–87; *Bulletin of the Ontario Hospitals for the Insane, 4*(1910[October]): 84–92; *Journal für Psychologie und Neurologie, 17*(1911) Ergänzungsheft (supplement issue): 427–431. (See an enlarged version: Jones, 1911).

Jones, E. (1910b). On the nightmare. *American Journal of Insanity, 66*: 383–417.

Jones, E. (1911). The action of suggestion in psychotherapy. *Journal of Abnormal Psychology, 5*: 217–254.

Jones, E. (1913). The relation between the anxiety neurosis and anxiety hysteria. *Journal of Abnormal Psychology, 8*: 1–9.

Jones, E. (1923a). The nature of auto-suggestion. *International Journal of Psychoanalysis, 4*: 293–312.

Jones, E. (1923b). *Essays in Applied Psycho-Analysis.* London: International Psycho-Analytic Press.

Jones, E. (1923c). Kälte, Krankheit und Geburt (Cold, illness and birth). *Internationale Zeitschrift für ärztliche Psychoanalyse, 9*: 260–265.

Jones, E. (1924a). Psycho-analysis and anthropology (Read before the Royal Anthropological Institute, London, 19 February 1924). *Journal of the Royal Anthropological Institute, 54*: 47–66.

Jones, E. (1924b). Review: "La Psychanalyse et les Névroses", by Dr. R. Laforgue & Dr. R. Allendy. Préface de M. Henri Claude. *International Journal of Psychoanalysis, 5*: 486–487.

Jones, E. (Ed.) (1924c). *Social Aspects of Psycho-Analysis; Lectures Delivered under the Auspices of the Sociological Society.* London: Williams & Norgate.

Jones, E. (1926). The development of psycho-analysis. *International Journal of Psychoanalysis, 7*: 103.

Jones, E. (1927a). James Glover 1882–1926. *International Journal of Psychoanalysis, 8*: 1–9.

Jones, E. (1927b). Review. Die Frage Der Laienanalyse. Unterredungen Mit Einem Unparteiischen: By Sigm. Freud. *International Journal of Psychoanalysis, 8*: 86–92.

Jones, E. (1928). *Psycho-Analysis*. London: E. Benn, 1928 [reprinted with an Addendum as *What is Psychoanalysis?* London: Allen & Unwin, 1949].

Jones, E. (1955). *The Life and Work of Sigmund Freud, Volume 2: Years of Maturity 1901–1919*. New York: Basic Books.

Jones, E. (1957). *The Life and Work of Sigmund Freud, Volume 3: The Last Phase 1919–1939*. New York: Basic Books.

Jones, E. (1959). *Free Associations. Memories of a Psycho-Analyst*. New York: Basic Books, 1959 [reprinted with a new introduction by Mervyn Jones. New Brunswick, NJ: Transaction, 1990].

Jones, E., & Balint, M. (2004). Correspondance Ernest Jones/Michael Balint. Traduite par Eva Brabant avec la collaboration de Marie Pierrakos. *Le Coq-Héron, 177*: 25–88.

Jung, C. G. (1912). *Psychology of the Unconscious: A Study of the Transformations and Symbolisms of the Libido: A Contribution to the History of the Evolution of Thought*. New York: Moffat, Yard. 1916.

King, P. (2003). The rediscovery of John Rickman and his work. In: *No Ordinary Psychoanalyst: The Exceptional Contributions of John Rickman* (pp. 1–68). London: Karnac.

King, P., & Steiner, R. (Eds.) (1991). *The Freud–Klein Controversies 1941–45*. London: Tavistock.

Kovács, M. M. (1994). *Liberal Professions and Illiberal Politics: Hungary from the Habsburgs to the Holocaust*. New York: Oxford University Press.

Kovács, V. (1936). Training and control analysis. *International Journal of Psychoanalysis, 17*: 346–354.

Krauss, F., & Brugsch, T. (Eds.) (1919–1928). *Spezielle Pathologie und Therapie innerer Krankheiten, 12 Volumes*. Berlin & Vienna: Urban & Schwarzenberg.

Laforgue, R., & Allendy, R. (1924). *La Psychanalyse et les Névroses*. Paris: Payot.

Leitner, M. (1998). *Freud, Rank und die Folgen. ein Schlüsselkonflikt für die Psychoanalyse*. Vienna: Turia + Kant.

Lieberman, E. J. (1984). *Acts of Will. The Life and Work of Otto Rank*. New York: Free Press.

Lieberman, E. J., & Kramer, R. (Eds.) (2012). *The Letters of Sigmund Freud & Otto Rank: Inside Psychoanalysis*, G. C. Richter (Trans.). Baltimore, MD: Johns Hopkins University Press.

Maddox, B. (2006). *Freud's Wizard. The Enigma of Ernest Jones*. London: John Murray.

Maeder, A. (1912). Über die Funktion des Traumes (On the function of dreams). *Jahrbuch für psychoanalytische und psychopathologische Forschungen, 4*: 692–707.

McGuire, W. (Ed.) (1994). *The Freud–Jung Letters: The Correspondence between Sigmund Freud and C. G. Jung*. Princeton, NJ: Princeton University Press.

Milner, M. (1954). Obituary: Karin Stephen 1889–1953. *International Journal of Psychoanalysis, 35*: 432–434.

Mitchell, T. W. (1938–1939). The contributions of psychical research to psychotherapeutics. *Proceedings of the Society for Psychical Research, 45*: 175–186.

Nitzschke, B. (1992). Wilhelm Stekel, ein Pionier der Psychoanalyse – Anmerkungen zu ausgewählten Aspekten seines Werkes. In: Ernst Federn & Gerhard Wittenberger (Eds.), *Aus dem Kreis um Sigmund Freud. Zu den Protokollen der Wiener Psychoanalytischen Vereinigung* (pp. 176–191). Frankfurt: Taschenbuch Verlag.

Nunberg, H., & Federn, E. (Eds.) (1974). *Minutes of the Vienna Psychoanalytic Society, Volume 4: 1912–1918*. New York: International Universities Press.

Paskaukas, A. R. (1993). *The Complete Correspondence of Sigmund Freud and Ernest Jones 1908–1939*. Cambridge, MA: Harvard University Press.

Payne, S. M. (1957). Dr. Ethilda Budgett-Meakin Herford. *International Journal of Psychoanalysis, 38*: 276–277.

Pfeifer, S. (1919). Äusserungen infantil-erotischer Triebe im Spiele (Psychoanalytische Stellungnahme zu den wichtigsten Spieltheorien) (Expressions of infantile-erotic drives in play (Psychoanalytic position regarding the most important theories of play)). *Imago, Zeitschrift für Anwendung der Psychoanalyse auf die Geisteswissenschaften, 5*(4): 243–282.

Rachman, A. W. (1997). The suppression and censorship of Ferenczi's Confusion of Tongues paper. *Psychoanalytic Inquiry, 17*: 459–485).

Rank, O. (1929)[1924]. *The Trauma of Birth*. London: Kegan Paul [reprinted with an introduction by E. J. Lieberman, New York: Dover, 1993].

Rickman, J. (1925). Abstract [on the "Zur Psychoanalyse der paralytischen Geistesstörung" (Psychoanalysis and the psychic disorders of general paresis) by Ferenczi & Hollós, 1922]. *British Journal of Medical Psychology, 5*(2): 120–126.

Rickman, J. (1933). Obituary: Sandor Ferenczi. *Proceedings of the Society for Psychical Research, 28*: 124–125.

Rickman, J. (Ed.) (1936). *On the Bringing Up of Children.* London: Kegan Paul [reprinted, London: Routledge, 2001].

Roazen, P. (1975). *Freud and His Followers.* New York: Knopf.

Roazen, P. (2000). *Oedipus in Britain. Edward Glover and the Struggle over Klein.* New York: Other Press.

Roazen, P., & Swerdloff, B. (1995). *Heresy: Sandor Rado and the Psychoanalytic Movement.* Northvale, NJ: Jason Aronson.

Robinson, K. (2002). The diaries of Claud Dangar Daly. *Bulletin of the British Psychoanalytic Society, 38*(4): 53–55.

Róheim, G. (1921). Das Selbst (The self). *Imago, Zeitschrift für Anwendung der Psychoanalyse auf die Geisteswissenschaften, 7*: 1–39, 142–179, 310–348, 453–504.

Róheim, G. (1925). *Australian Totemism. A Psychoanalytic Study in Anthropology.* London: Allen & Unwin.

Rolnik, E. J. (2012). *Freud in Zion: Psychoanalysis and the Making of Modern Jewish Identity.* London: Karnac.

Rudnytsky, P. L. (1991). *The Psychoanalytic Vocation: Rank, Winnicott, and the Legacy of Freud.* New Haven, CT: Yale University Press.

Rudnytsky, P. L. (2000). Enid Balint: the broken couch. In: *Psychoanalytic Conversations: Interviews with Clinicians, Commentators, and Critics* (pp. 1–26). Hillside, NJ: Analytic Press.

Rudnytsky, P., Bókay, A., & Giampieri, P. (Eds.) (1996). *Ferenczi's Turn in Psychoanalysis.* New York: New York University Press.

Sachs, H. (1925). Das Truma der Geburt und seine Bedeutung für die Psychoanalyse: by Otto Rank (1924). *International Journal of Psychoanalysis, 6*: 499–508.

Schröter, M. (1996). Zur Frühgeschichte der Laienanalyse. *Psyche, 50*(12): 1127–1175.

Schröter, M. (Ed.) (2004). *Sigmund Freud und Max Eitingon: Briefwechsel 1906–1939* (2 volumes). Tübingen: edition diskord.

Schröter, M. (2009). Freuds Memorandum "Soll die Psychoanalyse an der Universität gelehrt werden?" Zur Wiederauffindung des verschollenen Originals. *Merkur, 63*: 599–609.

Schur, M. (1972). *Freud: Living and Dying.* New York: International Universities Press.

Slade, T. K. (1923). *Our Phantastic Emotions: An Attempt To Suggest a Fresh Stand-point from which To View Human Activities.* London: Kegan Paul.

Steiner, R. (1991). To explain our point of view to English readers in English words. *International Review of Psycho-Analysis, 18*: 351–392.

Stekel, W. (1908). *Nervöse Angstzustände und ihre Behandlung. Mit einem Vorworte von Professor Dr. Sigmund Freud*. Berlin: Urban & Schwarzenberg, 1908 [2nd revised edn, 1912].

Stekel, W. (1926). On the history of the analytical movement. In: J. Bos & L. Groenendijk (Eds.), *The Self-Marginalization of Wilhelm Stekel. Freudian Circles Inside and Out* (pp. 131–162). New York: Springer-Verlag, 2007.

Stephen, K. (1934). Introjection and projection: guilt and rage. *British Journal of Medical Psychology, 14*(4): 316–331.

Stephen, K. (1939). Aggression in early childhood. *British Journal of Medical Psychology, 18*(2): 178–190.

Suttie, I. D. (1935). *The Origins of Love and Hate* (Preface by Dr J. A. Hadfield). London: Kegan Paul, 1935 [reprinted, London: Free Association Books, 1988].

Thomson, M. (2011). The solution to his own enigma: connecting the life of Montague David Eder (1865–1936), socialist, psychoanalyst, Zionist and modern saint. *Medical History, 55*: 61–84.

Timms, E. (Ed.) (1995). *Freud and the Child Woman: The Memoirs of Fritz Wittels*. New Haven, CT: Yale University Press.

Tomlison, W. C. (2010). Sandor Rado and the fate of the Berlin model in New York. *Psychoanalysis and History, 12*(1): 97–106.

Wittels, F. (1924). *Sigmund Freud. Der Mann, die Lehre, die Schule*. Leipzig: E. P. Tal.

Wittenberger, G. (1995). *Das "Geheime Komitee" Sigmund Freuds, Institutionalisierungsprozesse in der "Psychoanalytischen Bewegung" zwischen 1912 und 1927* [Sigmund Freud's "Secret Committee". Processes of institutionalisation within the "Psychoanalytic Movement" between 1912 and 1927]. Tübingen: edition diskord.

Wittenberger, G., & Tögel, C. (Eds.) (1999). *Die Rundbriefe des "Geheimen Komitees", Band 1, 1913–1920* (The circular letters of the "Secret Committee" Volume 1. 1913–1920). Tübingen: edition diskord.

Wittenberger, G., & Tögel, C. (Eds.) (2001). *Die Rundbriefe des "Geheimen Komitees", Band 2: 1921* (The circular letters of the "Secret Committee" Volume 2. 1921). Tübingen: edition diskord.

Wittenberger, G., & Tögel, C. (Eds.) (2003). *Die Rundbriefe des "Geheimen Komitees", Band 3: 1922* (The circular letters of the "Secret Committee" Volume 3. 1922). Tübingen: edition diskord.

Wittenberger, G., & Tögel, C. (Eds.) (2006). *Die Rundbriefe des "Geheimen Komitees", Band 4: 1923–1927* (The circular letters of the "Secret Committee" Volume 4. 1923–1927). Tübingen: edition diskord.

INDEX

For Product Safety Concerns and Information please contact our EU representative GPSR@taylorandfrancis.com Taylor & Francis Verlag GmbH, Kaufingerstraße 24, 80331 München, Germany